AF208001

INSTITUT FÜR AFRIKASTUDIEN

The peer-reviewed series "Bayreuth Studies in Politics and Society in Africa" publishes research about socio-political processes and structures in African societies. The editors welcome innovative monographs and guest edited volumes in either English or German which discuss historical and current transformations in African countries with an empirical or theoretical focus. The series is open to case studies and comparative research from the social sciences and related academic disciplines.

Bayreuther Studien zu Politik und Gesellschaft in Afrika
Bayreuth Studies in Politics and Society in Africa

is edited by

Institut für Afrikastudien (IAS) der Universität Bayreuth
Dr. Antje Daniel
Prof. Dr. Alexander Stroh

Volume 10

Asaf Augusto

North to South Migration

Portuguese Labour Migration to Angola

 **Nomos**

Funded by the Deutsche Forschungsgemeinschaft (DFG, German Research Foundation) under Germany's Excellence Strategy – EXC 2052/1 – 390713894.

The Deutsche Nationalbibliothek lists this publication in the Deutsche Nationalbibliografie; detailed bibliographic data are available on the Internet at http://dnb.d-nb.de

a.t.: Bayreuth, Univ., BIGSAS, Diss., 2020

ISBN   978-3-8487-8266-6 (Print)
            978-3-7489-2066-3 (ePDF)

British Library Cataloguing-in-Publication Data
A catalogue record for this book is available from the British Library.

ISBN   978-3-8487-8266-6 (Print)
            978-3-7489-2066-3 (ePDF)

Library of Congress Cataloging-in-Publication Data
Augusto, Asaf
North to South Migration
Portuguese Labour Migration to Angola
Asaf Augusto
177 pp.
Includes bibliographic references.

ISBN   978-3-8487-8266-6 (Print)
            978-3-7489-2066-3 (ePDF)

Onlineversion
Nomos eLibrary

1st Edition 2021
© Nomos Verlagsgesellschaft, Baden-Baden, Germany 2021. Overall responsibility for manufacturing (printing and production) lies with Nomos Verlagsgesellschaft mbH & Co. KG.

To my lovely wife
Sonja Augusto

Table of Contents

List of Figures

Acronyms

CPLP	Comunidade dos Países de Língua Portuguesa – Community of Portuguese Language Countries
EU	European Union
FNLA	Frente Nacional de Libertação de Angola – The National Front for the Liberation of Angola
IOM	International Organization for Migration
MPLA	Movimento Popular de Libertação de Angola – The People's Movement for the Liberation of Angola
PIDE	Polícia Internacional e de Defesa do Estado – International and State Defence Police
UNITA	União Nacional para a Independência Total de Angola – National Union for the Total Independence of Angola
USA	United States of America
UK	United Kingdom

Abstract

The economic crisis which has affected the southern EU countries since 2008 set in motion new migration trends. In the case of Portugal, post-crisis migration has been in two main directions: northwards to the more prosperous European countries and southwards to former Portuguese colonies in Africa, notably the oil-producing state of Angola. This thesis looks at Portuguese migration to Angola as a North-South migration and combines different theoretical frameworks to explain the dynamics involved. Concepts relevant to this migration include the notions of Portugal as 'semi-peripheral' within European and global migration systems. In spite of Portugal's position within the global migration system, this thesis demonstrates that Portugal's colonial legacy – especially 'Lusotropicalism' and 'coloniality' – plays a significant role in defining this migration as North-South. Moreover, concepts such as power geometry and uneven geographies of development are useful to explain this migration. Portuguese migrants in Angola enjoy a certain ethnic capital, particularly in Lubango, where my field research was carried out, because they are white and come from Europe. In other respects, too, the intersection between past and present is important to understand this migration. Discursively this migration is dominated by several myths, such as that of the Portuguese work ethic, the myth of the 'lazy native' and the myth of skills-based migration. These myths are used as justification for why Portuguese migrants, even in cases where they are less skilled, still enjoy certain advantages and privileges in comparison to their Angolan colleagues.

Acknowledgements

First, I would like to show my profound appreciation for the support provided by my supervisor Prof. Dr Martin Doevenspeck. I am grateful that he agreed to supervise my thesis and provide office space here at the University of Bayreuth and for being willing to provide the financial support letters when they were needed. Second, I am extremely grateful for the fundamental supervision work of Prof. Dr Russell King, University of Sussex, UK. I have to mention that he not only supervised the work despite the distance from Bayreuth but he tolerated my many incomplete drafts and read bits of the thesis on numerous occasions. I appreciate the incredible support from Mrs Jenny Money, formerly of the University of Sussex, UK. Aside from editorial support and encouragement to continue writing, she hosted me when I visited Prof. Dr Russell King in Sussex. Next, I would like to thank Prof. Dr Jorge Malheiros, University of Lisbon, Portugal, who provided important literature on Lusotropicalism and African migrants in Portugal.

I am also grateful to the Bayreuth International Graduate School of African Studies (BIGSAS) for providing financial support for this study and a stipend. I equally appreciate the fantastic support of the BIGSAS administration. This thesis could not have happened without the wonderful support of family and friends. Special praise goes to my lovely wife, Sonja Augusto, and my active boys, Jonathan Augusto and Samuel Augusto. They made important sacrifices so that I could be away for fieldwork and spend long hours in the office. My father, the Rev'd José Augusto, and my mother, Mrs. Joaquina Noé Augusto, have been supportive from both near and afar. My in-laws, Klaus and Angela Schmidt, as well Ms Barbara Schiessl, have provided different forms of support for which I am forever grateful. I also appreciate my numerous BIGSAS colleagues for the lively discussions that inspired me to think beyond my field of research. I would, in addition, like to extend my gratitude to Dr Serawit Debele, Dr Matthew Sabbi, Dr Gilbert Shang Ndi, Dr Florian Stoll, Paddy Kinyera, Kamal Donko, Julian Hollstegge and Alžběta Šváblová.

Chapter 1: Introduction and research aims

1.1 Why study Portuguese migration to Angola?

In the grand scheme of contemporary global migration, the recent flow of Portuguese migrants to Angola seems at first sight an anomaly. In popular discourse about migration, including political rhetoric, policy debates and the media, the main challenge of global migration is portrayed to be migration from the global South to the global North and how to control or stop it. In the United States, the main 'threat' of migration is seen to come from Mexico and the rest of Central and South America; in Europe it is migration from Africa that dominates the discussion, especially in Southern Europe. It is true that, within the overall total of 272 million for the global 'stock' of international migrants in 2019 (IOM 2020), the majority originate from the global South – between 70 and 80 per cent according to different estimates (by the World Bank, the United Nations Population Division and the United Nations Development Programme; see IOM 2013). However, such figures only tell part of the story and several caveats and nuances need to be drawn out. The first is that recording migration is a statistical minefield and much migration goes unrecorded, partly because of the uncertainty over who, exactly, is defined as a migrant. By the same token, the numbers of migrants are also often inflated, for political reasons. Second, international migration flows *within* the global South are almost as high as those from the South to the North. There are also substantial flows within the global North and from the North to the South, albeit smaller than those that originate from, or stay within, the global South. Third, the evolving pattern of global flows shows a mix of features which are constant over time (notably the movement of migrants from poor to richer countries) and those which are more ephemeral, driven by changes in the relative economic circumstances of countries and by opportunities which open up for migrants to improve their lives. This latter circumstance helps to explain the – at first sight, counterintuitive – recent migration of Portuguese to Angola, although there are other influences also at work – as this thesis will later reveal – to do with (post-)colonial relationships.

Having set up the 'problem question' of the thesis, this chapter provides an introduction to and an overview of the thesis, including further details on context, a specification of the research aims and questions and a chapter-by-chapter summary. It is also worth pointing out at this preliminary juncture that this thesis draws its inspiration and ethos from the rich interdisciplinary field of migration studies and, in particular, from the work of geographers in this field.

Migration has become one of the most pressing issues of our time, especially in developed countries; there is no day or week that goes by without hearing about migration. Academics, politicians, newspapers and pundits are constantly reporting about migration in relation to economic benefits or pressures, national security, demographic changes, integration and so on. As civil wars, famine and a lack of economic opportunity continue to ravage parts of the developing world, constant movement at various scales – inter-state, inter-city, inter-continental – has become a common fixture in what Castles and Miller (2009) have famously called the 'age of migration'.

The age of migration is characterised by constant mobility, transnational activities and political and economic instabilities that encourage new migration flows. It is also dominated by newly emerging concepts and theories that tend to prioritise certain migration processes over others. As this thesis will show, one of these incongruences in migration theory is the dominance of discourses on migration in developed countries, with much less attention paid to what goes on in the global South (Bakewell 2009).

In very simple terms, the global system is divided between North and South. The North is the domain of rich, industrialised, modern, developed and politically stable countries with prosperous economies and some kind of welfare state. The South, on the other hand, is the realm of poor countries which are politically unstable and which are characterised by extreme inequality and underdeveloped or developing economies. Countries in the South are generally perceived as not having the social, economic and political attributes to attract migrants from rich countries, while those in the North are considered to have the economic and political conditions that *do* attract migrants. As such, migration researchers have directly and indirectly concentrated their efforts on exploring South-North migration. These crude divisions of North and South are arbitrary, even though they might be useful to indicate the global scale of different geographical developments as well as the assertion of power and dominance of certain regions over the others (Williams, Meth and Willis 2014). However, it is worth noting that the North-South division should not be over-essentialised, because there are parts of the North that are poor and parts of the South that are rich (Williams *et al.* 2014). Furthermore, as Atkinson (2015) points out, inequality is also a growing phenomenon in countries in the global North where, on the one hand, governments are involved in cutting social programmes through economic austerity policies and, on the other, the accumulation of wealth by the super-rich goes unfettered.

Contrary to the dominant scholarship on migration that privileges movements from the South to the North, this thesis investigates the dynamics of migration from the North to the South, focusing in particular on Portuguese migration to Angola, which I conceptualise in this thesis as an example of North-South migration. Even though Portugal is located in the global North, it is not necessarily a country that can be considered economically well-off compared to those like Germany, France, the UK, Switzerland or the Scandinavian countries. As I shall demonstrate throughout the thesis, poverty, wealth and development are relative concepts and countries thus have changing relationships with each other as they assume different positionalities *vis-à-vis* each other in the global economic system – with consequences also for migration trends.

In order to understand recent Portuguese migration to Angola, it is important to look at the origins of this migration, which is linked to the economic crisis of 2008 which severely affected the Southern EU countries, especially Portugal, Spain and Greece and somewhat less so Italy. This economic crisis in turn set in motion new migration trends (Lafleur and Stanek 2017a). Since Portugal suffered considerably from the crisis, this ignited new migration dynamics. Given the historical propensity of Portuguese citizens to emigrate, Pereira and Azevedo (2019) see Portuguese migration to Angola as part of the 'fourth wave' of emigration, consequent upon the 2008 economic crisis and the austerity policies that followed in its wake.

According to Pereira and Azevedo's historical typology, the first wave lasted from 1850 until 1930 and saw most Portuguese migrants going to Brazil. Portuguese migration to Brazil was dominated by skilled migrants who wanted to settle permanently in the host country (Van der Waals 2011). The second wave took place between 1950 and 1974, ending with the fall of the Portuguese dictatorship and the onset of the first oil crisis in Europe. During this period, Portugal was one of the main suppliers of migrant workers to Western Europe's industrial powers, especially France and Germany. At the same time, there were considerable outflows to other destinations: the USA, Canada, Brazil, Venezuela, South Africa, Angola and Mozambique. During this period, Angola experienced considerable economic growth and it was also the period when oil was discovered. From 1950 to 1955, Portuguese migration to Angola increased by 80 per cent, with migrants arriving at the rate of 1,000 a month at the end of this growth period (Van der Waals 2011). The Portuguese colonial government offered subsides to new migrants, in particular those who were willing to settle in rural areas, because it was assumed that the 'white' presence there would speed up the 'civilisation' of the 'natives' (Bender 2004). However, the scheme turned out to be a failure because the new migrants were predominantly unskilled and preferred to settle in urban areas. This settlement was also problematic because the new migrants had to compete for jobs that were reserved for 'assimilated blacks' and Angolans of mixed race (Bender 2004). Yet new migrants were often favoured because of the colour of their skin and were paid more than black Angolans because they were considered 'civilised' by virtue of their birth in Portugal, even though many were illiterate (Bender 2004; Van der Waals 2011). It is not surprising that such discriminatory attitudes heightened the racial tension in urban areas in Angola and was one of the occurrences that ignited a pro-independence movement which, ironically, came from those very groups that had benefited educationally from the Portuguese colonial system (Malaquias 2007). These groups included progressive white Angolans, Angolans of mixed race and black Angolans (Mabeko-Tali 2018).

The third cycle started with the transition to democracy in Portugal and lasted into the new millennium. The same period witnessed the achievement of independence for Portugal's African colonies, including Angola. This phase was characterised by mixed flows, including emigration, immigration and return migration from earlier waves of emigration. Particularly dramatic was the repatriation of half a million Portuguese from the newly independent African colonies during 1974–75; 61 per cent of these *retornados* were from Angola. Later, Portuguese accession to the European Union in 1986 led to both a renewed emigration to more prosperous EU countries and Switzerland and a surge in immigration, initially from the so-called PALOP countries (Portuguese-speaking former African colonies – Angola, Cape Verde, Guinea-Bissau, Mozambique, São Tomé and Príncipe) and later from Eastern Europe (principally Ukraine, Moldova and Romania). Commenting on African migrants in Portugal, Fikes (2009) remarks that this was the period when Portugal enjoyed significant economic growth and African migration became more visible there. There was a sense that Portugal had now become part of the 'European club' of rich countries (Fikes 2009), part of whose wealth attracted diverse flows of international migrants, both skilled and unskilled, who played a part in enhancing this prosperity.

The circumstances framing Portugal's multi-directional fourth wave of emigration – northwards to richer, more recession-proof European countries, westwards to Brazil and southwards to Angola and Mozambique – were a direct result of the sharp contraction of the Portuguese economy after 2008 and the profound transformations of the national labour market brought about by austerity measures. The scale of the outflow rose to 115,000 per year during 2013–15, close to the annual average recorded during the peak years of postwar mass migration – 126,000 during 1965–73. According to data from the Portuguese National Statistics Institute summarised by Marques and Góis (2017), the economy shrank by an average of 1.7 per cent per year between 2009 and 2013, whilst unemployment – 7.6 per cent in 2008 – rose to 16.2 per cent in 2013 and even higher for younger people. Rising unemployment was accompanied by falling wages and decreasing job security. Unemployment benefits and other social welfare payments were also cut. Austerity policies were combined with a political rhetoric encouraging emigration. Unemployed young people were urged to 'leave their comfort zone' and 'go beyond our frontiers' to find better opportunities. Prime Minister Passos Coelho, head of the conservative coalition, suggested that unemployed schoolteachers should move to Portuguese-speaking countries such as Angola or Brazil to 'grasp the opportunities of the Portuguese language market' (Pereira and Azevedo 2019: 12). Opposition parties condemned such statements.

The constellation of primarily negative economic push factors from the Portuguese side was complemented by pull factors from the fast-growing Angolan economy. Two factors emerge as paramount, as pointed out by Candeias, Malheiros, Marques and Liberato (2019). The first was the end of the long-running civil war between the MPLA (People's Movement for the Liberation of Angola) and UNITA (The National Union for the Total Independence of Angola) and the restoration of peace in 2002. Economic growth was stimulated by rebuilding the country's damaged infrastructure and this created opportunities for both foreign investment and immigration. Secondly, natural resources, primarily exported oil, provided the foreign exchange needed to underwrite economic expansion. Angola is the fifth-largest oil producer in the world and the second in Africa after Nigeria. Quoting various sources, Candeias *et al.* (2019: 209–238) noted that oil production accounted for 91–98 per cent of Angola's exports by value during the years 2008–12 and for around 80 per cent of the country's total fiscal revenue. For a time, Angola was one of the fastest-growing economies in the world, with a 22 per cent annual growth rate during 2005–07.

Growth stalled during the global economic recession but then made a comeback after 2010 before stalling again in 2016.

There is a third factor which is germane, also noted by Candeias *et al.* (2019) – the intensity of the colonial relationship between the two countries. Angola was Portugal's oldest and largest colony in Africa, considered 'the jewel in the crown' of Portuguese colonial enterprise; it was also the last colony to attain independence, on 11 November 1975. Angola had experienced a large influx of Portuguese colonial settlers during the 1950s and 1960s, most of whom repatriated to Portugal following independence, as noted above. However, a small number of businesspeople and shopowners stayed on as 'white Angolans', making the new country their permanent home. It is important to point out as well that, at the time, there were white Angolans who had been living in Angola for more than three generations, in particular those living in coastal areas such as Luanda, Benguela and Namibe (Bender 2004). There were also a number of white and mixed-race Angolans who were part of the anti-colonial movement, with strong associations with the MPLA and who later occupied key positions of power within the postcolonial government (Mabeko-Tali 2018). Ironically, the current governor of Lubango, the place where this research was conducted, is a white Angolan businessman and some of the Portuguese participants in my research work for his construction company, *Omatapalo*.

Although Angola experienced remarkable economic growth after the end of the civil war in 2002, many social and political problems continued to affect the majority of the population. This social reality makes the study of migration to Angola interesting when trying to understand the paradoxes of Portuguese migration to Angola, a country where the everyday life of ordinary citizens is still framed by struggles to make ends meet. Unemployment in Angola ranges from 25 to 30 per cent and the majority of the population works in the informal sector of the economy; massive inequality persists and Angola continues to have one of the highest rates of infant mortality in the world (Soares de Oliveira 2015). Furthermore, the majority of the Angolan population still lives on less than two dollars a day, the educational and health services are still struggling to cater to every Angolan, the political system is dominated by an oligarchy-like system (Schubert 2017) and, lastly, there is an ongoing latent conflict in the oil-producing enclave of Cabinda, where separatists are campaigning for independence. These social and economic features of Angola constitute the paradoxical reality of a country with huge inequalities which are not the typical characteristics of a migrant-receiving country. Therefore, studying this migration trend is important because it demonstrates that the current global migration scenario contains dynamics that are less normative and predictable. Also, Portuguese migration to Angola presents a case where rationalist and determinist migration theories and concepts can be problematised by viewing migration as a complex intersection of processes and disciplines. Subjects like history, human geography, sociology, social anthropology, economics and politics can all be useful in understanding the trajectory of Portuguese migration to Angola from different angles, especially when insights and theories from these different disciplines are combined together.

Portuguese migration to Angola is also one of the few cases where former European colonists are migrating to former colonies in sub-Saharan Africa in search of economic opportunity after the end of colonialism. With the exception of South Africa and Namibia, such migration has not happened in post-independence sub-Saharan Africa on the same scale as the current Portuguese migration to Angola (Åkesson 2018). The general understanding is that Africa does not have the necessary political and economic conditions to attract European migrants and those Europeans who do venture to go to Africa are going there in order to help to develop the continent and not to seek personal economic opportunity. Equally, as I shall demonstrate later, the empirical evidence shows that a similar discourse of going to Africa in order to 'help' is held by some of the Portuguese migrants in Angola, who see their migration trajectory as that of an aid worker or a developer. Such a discourse of 'benevolent Portuguese' seems to fit with the social conditions of Angola, fraught still with the challenges of postwar reconstruction and profound inequality.

In light of the reasons mentioned above, this study argues that Portuguese migration to Angola should be understood not only as a result of the economic crisis[1] or as a skills-driven migration but also as a complex web of intersections that include the Portuguese colonial and postcolonial

---

1 The dominant understanding of Portuguese migration to Angola tends to focus on three aspects: first, the economic crisis in Portugal and subsequent youth unemployment and austerity measures (Glorious and Dominguez-Mujica 2017; Pereira and Azevedo 2019). Second, there is a strong emphasis on the discourse of skills-based Portuguese migration to Angola (Candeias *et al.* 2019). Third, other studies focus on the role of Portuguese companies in the reconstruction of the Angolan infrastructure after years of civil war (Soares de Oliveira 2015). All these approaches tend to somehow prioritise the relevance of the economic aspects of this migration. However, this thesis demonstrates that there is more to Portuguese migration to Angola than the economic crisis, skills and reconstruction of the Angolan infras-

legacy, family networks, discourses and myths, issues of trust and representation and the phenomena of Eurocentrism, 'race'[2] and coloniality. These concepts are directly and indirectly linked to Portuguese migration to Angola and play a significant role in our understanding of some of the dynamics involved in this migration trajectory. Dynamics such as the postcolonial construction of Portuguese migrants to Angola as a skill-based migration can only be understood in the light of the Portuguese colonial myth. Portuguese colonialism in Angola was dominated by several myths, such as that of the 'lazy native', which promoted Portuguese interests and excluded black Angolans (Bender 2004). In postcolonial Angola, this myth persists and is used, in some cases, as justification for the preference for Portuguese workers in Angola. The notion that things in Angola only work well once a Portuguese is in charge speaks of lingering colonial nostalgia in the country. It is a well-known reality that the Angolan postcolonial economy was dominated by shortages of skilled workers which forced the postcolonial government to rely on Cuban, Eastern European, Vietnamese and Russian professionals (Hatzky 2012; Malaquias 2007). However, there are four key aspects that make the Portuguese migration to Angola especially interesting. The first is the coloniality aspect, by which is meant the acceptance of Portuguese cultural etiquette and the Portuguese language as signs of civilisation. Second is the association of Portuguese migration with skills-based migration only, which is far from the truth. Third, the association of this migration only from an economic angle exemplifies another limitation. The economic aspect plays a significant role in understanding Portuguese migration to Angola, for there is a need to account for other factors beside the economic imperative. The combination of factors needs to be analysed in order to have a better picture of these migration processes. Fourth, the negation of the colonial legacy in particular family networks (both white and mixed-race Angolans) and the role of

---

tructure. I argue that Portuguese migration to Angola is also linked to the Portuguese colonial legacy there – a legacy that continues to shape employment and job opportunities in Angola.

2   This thesis uses a definition of race and racism based on Portuguese colonialism. According to Jerónimo (2015), the definition of racism and race under Portuguese colonialism was not limited to skin pigmentation only but also included the attribution of certain negative character traits based on civilisation hierarchy. In other words, the definition is linked to what Bonilla-Silva (2006) called racism without race, which manifests itself in the form of a negative cultural discourse that rationalises unjust practices.

'race' in Portuguese migration to Angola constitute further key aspects of the 'story' of this migration.

1.2 Research aims and questions

This study seeks both to contribute to the scholarly field of migration studies by presenting an unusual and original case of European-based migration to Africa and to engage theoretically and empirically with some of the dynamics involved in this migration. Within this overall claim to originality, the thesis has four broad aims.

First, it aims to analyse the characteristics and complexities of Portuguese migration to Angola in light of the economic and social realities both of Angola and of the economic crisis in Portugal. Furthermore, the study also aims at analysing other factors that contribute to this migration beyond economic ones, notably those that are connected to Portuguese colonialism and its legacies in Angola.

Second, the thesis critically analyses and engages with the relevant migration theories – in particular, normative and determinist theories – and relates their normativity to the case of Portuguese migration to Angola. The emphasis here is to challenge the conventional assumptions that arise from South-North migration which are hegemonic in migration studies. Borrowing from theories such as those of the South, postcolonial studies and coloniality, the thesis aims to problematise Portuguese migration to Angola against the backdrop of the dominant South-North understanding of international migration and to present a case that does not fit the typical South-North conceptualisation of why global migration takes place.

Third, the thesis aims to analyse the myths and realities surrounding skills-based Portuguese migration to Angola. Key here is the role of the representation of the South in order to interrogate the Orientalist and Eurocentric North-South paradigm of 'expat' migration.

Fourth, the thesis aims to present original and rigorous empirical findings based on responses obtained from in-depth interviews and participant observation with Portuguese migrants and Angolans. In particular, emphasis is placed on the privileges that Portuguese migrants have in Angola because of the fact that they come from a supposedly 'civilised' continent and country as well as how this is linked to race, the postcolonial legacy and coloniality.

Therefore the thesis asks the following two basic questions – the first theoretical and the second empirical:
- How can recent Portuguese migration to Angola be 'explained'?[3]
- What are the distinctive characteristics of this migration flow?

These overall framing questions can be broken down into a series of more specific sub-questions.

a) What theoretical perspectives help us to understand Portuguese migration to Angola?
b) What are the details and dynamics at play in this migration (historical, political, economic, cultural, institutional, spatio-temporal etc.)?
c) What is the relationship between the realities of Portuguese employment in Angola and the prevalent discourses and myths about the Portuguese and Angolans?
d) Does being a Portuguese migrant in Angola have an advantage for employment in the country?
e) What is the role of skill in this migration? How are skilled and unskilled Portuguese able to obtain employment on the Angolan labour market?
f) How do Angolan nationals respond to the presence of Portuguese migrants in Angola?

The above listings of aims and questions are obviously specific to my investigation in this thesis but they also raise a broader 'knowledge' question about the different disciplines that study migration – economics, geography, sociology, political science, anthropology and so on. As most migration scholars point out (for some authoritative voices, see Brettel and Hollifield 2008; Castles and Miller 2009; Cohen 1995), migration is a richly interdisciplinary field of study and much of the best research and scholarship on migration combines theoretical and analytical insights from several disciplines. Indeed Favell (2008), in an inspiring essay, argues for Migration Studies as a 'postdisciplinary' field of study. Favell also writes in praise of geography – 'arguably the most exciting discipline in the social sciences' (2008: 262) – as the most flexible approach to studing the phenomenon of migration. Both geography and migration, he points out, are fundamentally concerned with space, place, flows, networks and transactions. My ap-

---

3 The emphasis acknowledges existing disciplinary explanations and perspectives on Portuguese migration to Angola. Moreover, this thesis does not dogmatically claim to offer the *only* explanation for Portuguese migration to Angola. Rather, it contributes to the debate through a different explanation with a clear focus on the Portuguese colonial legacy and its symbolic presence.

proach in this thesis, then, is to follow the dual approach indicated by Favell (2008) and developed further by King (2012), which is both to regard migration as an interdisciplinary (or, indeed, postdisciplinary) field of study and to regard (human) geography as my natural disciplinary home for this migration research, not least because geography is, itself, a broad and open discipline.

1.3 Setting the scene: facts and figures on Portuguese migration to Angola

Obtaining data on Portuguese migration to Angola can be a daunting exercise. Data are imprecise on the scale of the recent Portuguese migration to Angola for several reasons. The most complex one is that Portuguese colonial history has bequeathed a legacy of strong family ties in Angola. Interracial marriages and liaisons created a hybrid mix of Portuguese-Angolan family connections; several Angolan families can still trace their Portuguese ancestry and many have dual nationality, which is obtainable through both maternal and paternal ancestry or through naturalisation. According to Soares de Oliveira (2015), some members of the Angolan elite have dual nationality. Besides this, there is also a small white Angolan community which is often overlooked when analysing Angolan social dynamics, due to the unconscious assumption that they are Portuguese and that no white people stayed on after independence. Some of the white Angolans, in particular the younger generation, also have dual nationality and, in some cases, live partially in Angola and partially in Portugal, depending on the economic performance of the two countries. Åkesson (2018) also points out that some of the Angolan whites who left as children in 1975 after independence are eligible for Angolan citizenship and some of the recent Portuguese migration to Angola is linked to this group. All the above makes it difficult to define who is and who is not Angolan and to evaluate the extent to which recent and current Portuguese migration to Angola is linked to these family histories. In some cases, there might be a link to these recent historical dynamics while, in others, not.

The second obstacle to obtaining good estimates is that it has been common practice for most migrants to work in Angola with only a tourist visa. This practice was widespread because of the bureaucratic challenges faced by Portuguese migrants applying for an Angolan work permit. Portuguese migrants would normally work for three months on a tourist visa and then apply for a further three months before returning to Portugal to apply for a work permit.

Thirdly – and related to the previous point – it is difficult to obtain information from the Angolan authorities on the number of Portuguese migrants in the country. There are Portuguese leaving Portugal as Portuguese and arriving in Angola as Angolans and there are Angolans leaving Angola as Angolans and arriving in Portugal as Portuguese. This makes it very difficult for the Angolan and Portuguese states to control who is coming in and who is leaving, at least on the criterion of nationality. On the other hand, doing statistical research in Angola is very challenging, a situation which other researchers (Åkesson 2016; Åkesson and Orjuela 2019; Candeias *et al.* 2019) attribute to the secret and corrupt nature of the Angolan state apparatus inherited from decades of civil war.[4]

Unsurprisingly, there is conflicting information on the number of Portuguese migrants in Angola. Costa, Teixeira Lopes and Louça (2014) suggest 'at least 200,000' but these authors provide no back-up details or methods for this estimate, so it is not clear if this figure includes dual nationals and/or workers operating on a tourist visa. Other estimates are lower. Candeias *et al.* (2019) reveal the discrepancy between the different sources. Portuguese Embassy and Consular registers show a growth in the number of Portuguese living in Angola from 72,706 in 2008 to 134,473 in 2015. Angolan Ministry of the Interior data for 2011 on foreigners with residence or work permits show that, of a total of 339,035, only 44,761 (13.2 per cent) were held by Portuguese, compared to 160,262 (47.3 per cent) by Chinese, 36,317 (10.7 per cent) by Brazilians and 15,694 (4.6 per cent) by South Africans.[5] The Portuguese Observatório de Emigração (2019) points out that, in 2016, there were 92,666 registered Portuguese migrants in Angola and 97,576 in 2017.

---

4 Schubert (2017) additionally points out that Angola, in particular, is one of the most difficult countries in Africa in which to collect data, partly because of its history of state colonial repression and its communist postcolonial regime. The people are constantly suspicious and fear sharing information, in particular information related to politics.

5 The number of Chinese work permits is higher than those of Portuguese migrants because Chinese migration to Angola is linked to Chinese government oil loans. The Angolan government provides oil to the Chinese government and, in return, Chinese companies are given contracts to rebuild the country (Schmitz 2018). However, although Chinese migration to Angola is numerically higher, the Chinese do not have the 'cultural capital' of the Portuguese. Furthermore, Schmitz (2018) points out that the Chinese in Angola do not have the same status as Europeans – there is a hierarchy in status, with European migrants being treated better than other migrants. Moreover, the Chinese migrants are mainly found in the construction sector while the Portuguese migrants are also spread across other sectors.

1.4 Overview of the thesis

The thesis is structured in six chapters. Here follows a brief summary of each chapter in turn. This introductory Chapter 1 has focused on the study's contextual background, justification for the research and the aims and research questions.

Chapter 2 critically engages with the migration literature. The main argument of the chapter is that existing migration theories have been dominated by South-North migration concepts at the expense of other migration dynamics. For example, South-South migration is a common migration channel – globally almost on a par with South-North migration in terms of numbers – but it does not feature nearly as much as South-North migration theory. This discrepancy often gives the impression that South-North is the only migration route which, in turn, produces the perception that migration theory is 'North-centric', implicitly seeing Europe and North America as the centre of the migration universe. In order to challenge this North-centric bias, this chapter uses 'theories of the South' such as postcolonialism and coloniality to understand North-South migration, in particular the issues of privilege, power and 'race'. These concepts help us to see how European migrants in the South are treated differently or as expatriates.

Chapter 3 is about methodology. It explains why some methods were used instead of others and why they suited the context in which this study was conducted. In-depth interviews, participant and general observation were mainly used and justification is given for why these methods were suitable for this kind of research. The chapter discusses my arrival in the field and some of the changes that I have observed over many years since the previous times I spent in Angola as well as some of the challenges in recruiting participants in a society divided by class and race. In order to have a proper understanding of the dynamics of Portuguese migration to Angola, the participants included Portuguese migrants, skilled Angolans working with Portuguese migrants, white Angolans and Angolan business-owners who employed Portuguese migrants. The participants included both men (the majority) and women. The second part of the research was conducted in Lisbon. The chapter recounts the challenges I faced when doing research there and especially the obstacles to recruiting participants. A brief characterisation and background of the participants, both in Lisbon and in Lubango (the city where I did my Angolan fieldwork), is presented as well as my variable positionality as a researcher in these two field-sites.

Chapters 4 and 5 are the two main empirical-results chapters. They are the two longest of the thesis and are its core in terms of originality. Chapter 4 deals with the background of Portuguese migration to Angola, set within the so-called Lusophone migration system. I also discuss the myth of Lusotropicalism – the Portuguese idea that there was something benevolently special about Portuguese colonialism – and link this controversial notion to some of my empirical findings. The myth of Lusotropicalism is a historical one that presents Portugal as an exceptional country in Europe, without racism and with the capacity to understand and integrate in Africa better than other European countries. This is visible in the claimed more culturally sensitive nature of the Portuguese colonial system which produced a number of mixed-race families. Lusotropicalism still manifests itself in various forms, in some cases as 'colour-blind' and in others as the Portuguese 'exceptionalist' ability to go anywhere and adapt. It is important to mention that the myth of Lusotropicalism is also held by many white, some black (assimilates) and some mixed-race Angolans.

Chapter 5 deals with the discourses around Portuguese migration to Angola, in particular the 'developmental' discourse that sees Portuguese migration to Angola as a means to help to develop the country rather than link the migration to the economic crisis in Europe. This discourse positions the Portuguese in Angola as the 'good migrants' who are there to rebuild the underdeveloped and war-ravaged country. The discourse of Portuguese migration to Angola is dominated by skills-based migration as well as the development rationale. The chapter critiques the Afro-pessimism which dominates part of Angolan society, in particular the notion of ongoing coloniality.

The final chapter, Chapter 6, is the conclusion, where I revisit the research questions and highlight the key findings and contributions of the thesis, both empirical and theoretical. The chapter also suggests further research on this topic and identifies some aspects of the thesis that were not fully addressed.

Chapter 2: Migration dynamics in the global North and South: Portuguese migration to Angola

2.1 Introduction

The previous chapter introduced the thesis – above all the research questions, the background context and a general overview of its contents. Chapter 2 seeks to review the literature, with a particular emphasis on the dynamics of North-South migration and the imbalance in global migration theory, in order to conceptualise other forms of migration that are not directly linked to the global North. The chapter deals with the prevailing Eurocentrism which puts Europe's social problems at the centre of the universe and ignores other social dynamics. The chapter also looks at some of the factors that contribute to neglecting the global South, in particular the Northern representation of the South as a place ravaged by backwardness and social problems. The dominant notion that the global South is sending and the global North is receiving migrants is also discussed. The case here is not to dispute the statistical evidence of migration flows or the economic problems of the South but, rather, to demonstrate that there is more to the South – and to Africa in particular – than the typical images presented in the North. Furthermore, Portuguese migration to Angola and the so-called Lusophone migration system are discussed in order to demonstrate the complexities of this migration system. Finally, this chapter deals with certain perspectives and myths – postcolonialism, coloniality, work ethics and social capital – as they relate to North-South migration dynamics.

2.2 Challenging the Northern bias in migration theory

Migration theories in the North have been dominated by three biased conceptualisations: the first is the reduction of North-South migration to the historical events of colonialism, the second is the over-emphasis on South-North migration and the third is the overall neglect of South-South and North-South migration dynamics.

2.2.1 The reduction of North-South migration to the historical events of colonialism

Since the end of colonialism, little or no attention has been given to the dynamics of North-South migration (Beauchemin 2018). The historical colonial analysis of North-South migration is primarily concerned with describing colonial excursions and settlements in parts of the South (Castles and Kosack 1973). The work of Connell (2007) is important in understanding the rationale for this migration, as it focuses on the philosophical assumptions that led to it. Some of these assumptions are still directly and indirectly associated with current North-South migration dynamics. One assumption was the belief that progress in the South could only be achieved with the presence of Europeans (Connell 2007). A good example is the controversial work of conservative historian Ferguson (2012) on 'civilisation', which praises the achievements of Europeans in the South in areas like education, health care and science. However, Ferguson ignores the atrocities committed in the name of civilisation and the limitations of colonialism. Civilisation was designed to include just a few 'natives' and exclude the majority. In other words, Ferguson (2012) does not seem to see that civilisation was designed to benefit a select few in the South and was not as noble as he suggests. Mignolo (2011) argues that there was a dark side to the colonial project of 'civilisation' which was preoccupied with the subjugation of the people in the South and left significant numbers of people disenfranchised. Parts of today's Latin America, Asia and Africa are still living the legacy of such 'civilisation'. For Mignolo (2011), the dark side of Western civilisation is the blindness which leads it to impose, subjugate and assimilate the South at any cost with no regard for the human impact. The discourses and practices of colonial migration from the North to the South under the myth of civilisation are not noble and need to be evaluated in the light of the other tragedies committed in the name of civilisation.

Besides the atrocities thus committed, Castles and Kosack (1973) point out that North-South colonial migration and settlement was motivated in some cases by the economic opportunities in the South. The economic crisis in the North, together with the lack of opportunity, was one of the major reasons why North-South colonial migration happened historically. In some cases, governments in the North played an active role in mobilising and financially subsidising Europeans to migrate to the South (Bender 2004; Castles and Kosack 1973). However, the historical discourse of this migration was loaded with the language of modernisation, such as the attitude of wanting to 'save' the South from backwardness and from obscurantism (Connell 2007). This is especially evident when it comes to understanding Africa, which was and still is viewed as backward, uncivilised, underdeveloped and in need of the political, economic and cultural transformation which only the North can offer through the South's political and cultural assimilation into a 'superior' civilisation (Bender 2004). During the colonial era, Europeans were perceived as having certain characteristics conducive to 'bringing up' the rest of the so-called uncivilised world to a decent level of civilisation (Mbembe 2001).

2.2.2 The overemphasis on South-North migration

Since North-South migration does not occur as frequently as it used to, historically, during the colonial era, there is an overemphasis on South-North migration which gives the impression that this is the only global migration flow of any importance. The migration literature and theory have been dominated by South-to-North migration, in particular to Western Europe, North America and Australasia (Castles and Miller 2009). This hegemonic paradigm has been dominated by the view that sees migration as driven primarily by economic factors, pushing migrants from the global South or from countries considered as poor, unstable and with serious social inequalities and pulling them towards the countries of the global North, considered rich and politically stable, with a strong middle class. It appears that international migration is the most visible in the global North although this is partly related to the location there of the majority of the world's migration scholars. Another factor could be the tendency to reduce most migration dynamics to economic factors without seeking other explanations. There is the tendency to elevate migration theories such as the neo-classical equilibrium approach, which tends to reduce migration to a phenomenon mainly induced by economic hardship (Castles and Miller 2009; de Haas 2008). In neo-classical theory, citizens from the South are depicted as desperately trying to flee dire economic conditions. In this line of thinking, migration is primarily economic and migrants from the South are perceived as wanting to maximise their income by migrating to the North in order to enjoy its prosperity.

Although neo-classical approaches put emphasis on the dominance of economic drivers as the primary cause of migration and on the willingness of migrants to work in order to maximise their income, the popular discourse in the North tends to link South-North migration to the welfare state. In other words, migrants are perceived as running away from deeply deprived to prosperous areas in order to benefit from welfare-state hand-outs (Dølvik 2013). The point here is not to show whether or not there is a connection between South-North migration and welfare; rather, it is to demonstrate the centrality of economics in South-North migration.

Neo-classical equilibrium theory has been challenged by less-determinist theories that try to provide a more nuanced understanding of migration. One such theory is transnationalism, which sees migration as a result not only of economic influences but also of a combination of various interactive factors (de Haas 2008). Unlike the neo-classical equilibrium theory, transnationalism sees the global South and North in constant interaction and cooperation (de Haas 2008; Glick Schiller and Faist 2010). In other words, migrants are in constant contact with their country of origin, which gives much more than a sense that the idea of migration is a one-sided affair. This contact is maintained through sending remittances and emails, making telephone calls and participating in cultural and religious events. Although transnationalism can help to see migration from different angles rather than just the perspective of economics, it still tends to be 'North-centric' because the North is viewed as a place where activities like the sending of remittances occurs; in contrast, the South is seen as a place where all the 'cultural' activities such as religious ceremonies happen. Smith's (2006) research on Mexican migrants in New York is a clear example of how the North serves as a place that provides remittances and the South as a place that provides cultural experiences. Smith's study is helpful in understanding how transnational dynamics unfold; however, it indirectly presents the South in this case as 'exotic' whereas the North – here the USA – is the provider of remittances.

Beauchemin's (2018) work on migration between Africa and Europe also uses transnationalism to understand the migration dynamics between these two continents. Beauchemin attempts to understand migration ostensibly from the perspectives of both Europe and Africa, looking at the factors that compel migrants to risk their lives in order to reach Europe. Concepts such as transit migration are also indirectly explored. However, the dynamics between Africa and Europe are actually those of African migrants in Europe, on whom the emphasis lies. Africa is conceptualised as sending migrants and Europe as receiving them. There is no reference to North-South migration, not even to so-called European expatriates in Africa. Migration is presented as a one-way street. Research by Beauchemin (2018) enables us to see the flow of migrants from Africa to Europe but it is dominated by the rationale that sees Europe as the receiving continent and Africa as a sending continent; such a rationale is helpful but it does not do justice to other contexts such as North-South or South-South migration, both of which are important in reality.

2.2.3 The neglect of South-South migration dynamics

According to Bakewell (2009), South-South migration is very common but less attention is given to it. Such neglect might be due to the obvious fact that intra-South migration has less impact in the North. In other words, the North is only preoccupied with migration flows that have a direct impact there. There is not much reference to the fact that countries in the South are also recipients of migrants – in particular of refugees. Yet, the reality of global migration patterns is somewhat different and requires a complementary view from the South (Castles and Delgado Wise 2008). It is true that, of the four global 'compass migrations', South-North is the largest although almost as many migrants move between countries of the global South; smaller but significant numbers also migrate North-to-North and North-to-South. For instance, as Crawley, Düvell, Jones, McMahon and Sigona (2018) argue, during the so-called migration crisis in 2015, countries like Turkey and Jordan took more refugees than all the EU countries combined but the backlash in the EU was far stronger than in Turkey and Jordan, leading to the rise of anti-migration political parties and to more-restricted polices.

According to Betts and Collier (2017), the majority of refugees end up staying in countries in the global South. There are several factors that contribute to this, one being geographical proximity, since most refugees and migrants tend to migrate to neighbouring countries (Bakewell 2009). Another factor is the existing rigid visa regime in the North, which makes it difficult for migrants to reach there. Moreover, there are also financial demands and many risks involved in attempting to reach the North (Crawley *et al.* 2018). Thus, not every migrant ends up reaching his or her preferred destination, often taking years and many setbacks before arriving somewhere in the North.

In spite of these obstacles, popular discourse in the North is fuelled with fears of invasion, drastic demographic changes and the replacement of 'white' Europeans by migrants, echoing what Smith (2019) calls the *scramble for Europe*. Such a discourse gives the impression that migration is only happening from South to North. Scholars like Kaplan (2000) predicted that migrants from the South, in particular Africa, would invade Europe and North America if nothing was done to ameliorate the economic condition of the continent of origin. Although such a prediction never materialised, Smith (2019) revived Kaplan's argument. For Smith, given the higher birth rate in Africa and the increased young population, African migrants would be a majority in Europe by 2050. His argument is based on African social problems in combination with the continent's population increase, which he uses as indicators of the so-called scramble for Europe. Ironically, the social problems that he mentioned are not new – they have been there for years. Moreover, the process of African migration to Europe does not depend only on those factors suggested by Smith (2019). Additionally, just as there is migration happening from South to North, there is also significant effort being made to restrict such migration. According to Vaughan-Williams (2015), governments in the North have been restricting migration to the extent of collaborating with some Southern governments that are notorious for human rights violations. These restrictions have prevented the flow of migrants from reaching the North and kept migrants in the South under inhumane conditions in so-called transit countries. The alarmist argument of Smith (2019) does not take into account how states in the North are countering the supposed surge in South-North migration, in particular through new regimes of deportation. His arguments serve to reinforce the myths of invasion, replacement and fear and, not surprisingly, nativist parties in the North have been mobilising around these myths, thereby reproducing a strong Eurocentric and Orientalist representation of the South.

2.3 South to North migration dynamics: Eurocentrism and Orientalism

The over-emphasis on South-North migration at the expense of other forms and routes of migration such as South-South has led some migration scholars to affirm that the migration literature has been dominated by Eurocentrism. Castles and Delgado Wise (2008) define Eurocentrism as the notion that the world revolves around Europe and North America; or what Chakrabarty (2000) called 'provincialising Europe' – making Europe and European history the centre of the universe. Eurocentrism can also be the reduction of global problems to European and North American ones. For example, when a catastrophe happens in Europe and North America, it is depicted in the media as 'abnormal' but when the same tragedy happens elsewhere it is not given the same prominence but, rather, is regarded as an endemic problem of less-developed countries (Shohat and Stam 1994).

Eurocentrism is dominated by a hierarchical worldview of geography, history, economics, politics and 'race' (Shohat and Stam 1994). It operates under a strong binary of differences. As such, Eurocentrism is too inflexible to acknowledge other realities outside of Europe and North America, particularly any that might challenge or question Eurocentric dominance. Eurocentrism is preoccupied with representing the rest of the world as being in total contrast to the North by constructing the rest as the 'other', a distant place without history, culture or future (Mudimbe 1988) – a place that needs to be reshaped economically, politically and culturally in order to be elevated to the standard of the North (Power 2006). The North is idealistically represented as a paradise on earth and a geographical entity that the South should attempt to emulate in its political and economic policies and experiments (Mbembe 2001). These dichotomies and contrasts are based on strong differentiations between superior and inferior, as summarised by Shohat and Stam (1994: 2):

> *Our* 'nation', *their* 'tribe'; *our* 'religion', *their* 'superstition'; *our* 'culture', *their* 'folklore'; *our* 'art', *their* 'artefacts'; *our* 'demonstrations', *their* 'riots'; *our* 'defence', *their* 'terrorism'.

In the Eurocentric worldview, there is no expectation that the South has anything of importance to contribute to the North apart from being a recipient of assistance (Mignolo 2011) and a supplier of migrant workers. Since the South is viewed as inferior, it is the duty of the North to bring the South up to its own economic, political and cultural standards. Such a duty operates more like the old colonial myth of the 'civilising mission' (Mbembe 2001).

Although the civilisation project was partially abandoned after the Second World War, the Eurocentric notion of superiority and power continues to dominate the interactions between the North and South (Shohat and Stam 1994). Ideas of power being solely concentrated in the North continue to linger through various forms of political, cultural and economic interventions which, in theory, are meant to help the South but which, in practice, are there to advance the interests of the North (Gopal 2013). One of the areas where the economic dominance of the North is more visible is in the imposition of policies such as structural adjustment and austerity that benefit the local elite, who tend to work closely with former colonialists (Bhabha and Comaroff 2002). The Eurocentric hegemony does not manifest itself solely through these differences but also extends to the old colonial stereotypes of laziness, welfare dependence, having too many children, criminality and so forth (Chavez 2008). These stereotypes are largely reserved for the countries of the South, especially as regards their inability to solve social problems such as poverty and unemployment.

In terms of difference, some of these Eurocentric assumptions stem from the idea that differences automatically lead to conflict (Sen 2006). Much of this view draws heavily on the Balkan conflict, the Rwandan genocide and other conflicts where differences of religion and ethnicity have led to violence and genocide. These examples are taken as given and assumed to be normative in any context. Sen (2006) points out that differences do not necessarily lead to clashes or conflict; there are countries that have lived together in harmony in spite of differences in culture, religion and ethnicity.

There is no better manifestation of Eurocentrism than the influential work of Huntington (1996). Huntington's book *The Clash of Civilizations* demonstrates how Eurocentrism operates, in particular when it comes to viewing how the people of different continents interact with one another based on 'civilisation'. He divides the globe into what he sees as different civilisations and puts groups that do not necessarily belong together in single and fixed categories just because they might come from the same country or region and rigidly attributes a 'civilisation' to them. In spite of this simplifying error, Huntington's Eurocentric approach has had a tremendous impact on the way in which international relations, ethnic studies, conflict studies and migration studies are undertaken (Sen 2006). Much of our current understanding and construction of migrants, especially those of African and Muslim descent, has been from the perspective of 'otherness' and an alleged 'clash of civilisations'. The assumption is that different ethnic and religious groups and their civilisations are so different that they cannot be integrated into Western civilisation. Huntington (2004) published a second work – *Who Are We?* – with a similar Eurocentric rationale as *The Clash of Civilizations*, this time applying the same logic to the growing number of Mexican migrants in North America. The main argument in Huntington's (2004) book is that Mexican migrants constitute a danger to American social cohesion because of their Catholic religion, too many children, inability to assimilate to the American way of life and lack of loyalty to America. Moreover, Huntington argues that American religion should remain Protestant, 'white' and Anglo-Saxon, an argument once again based on the narrow notion that the South cannot be 'integrated' into the North because the South is so different. The interesting observation here is how Mexican migrants are represented as a homogenous inferior group based on their Mexican Catholic culture. In other words, the driving element of Eurocentrism is the difference of geography or, rather, of uneven geographies and the notion that the problems of the South would automatically be transferred to the North given the disparity of economic conditions between Mexico and the United States.

Certain regions of the South are indeed ravaged by war, famine, high infant mortality and unemployment as well as political and economic instability. This is the reality in parts of Latin America, most of Africa and parts of Asia. However, the Eurocentric representation of the South becomes unreliable once the problems of the South become the only lens through which to understand the reality there and once the direct and indirect involvement of the North in creating problems in the South is ignored as part of the analysis. It is clear that the South is not only dominated by social problems. For example, there is more to the South than simply the images of desperate migrants attempting to enter the North. The South is complex and diverse, not homogenous as Eurocentric views tend to depict it (Power 2006). Also, some of the political and economic problems of the South are directly linked to the North's interests there which, in some cases, are what generate new flows of migrants – in particular of refugees. A good example could be the migration flows from Iraq, Afghanistan, Libya and Syria. Movements from these countries are the direct result of policies like the war on terror and regime changes which ignited and exacerbated instability in the region. Migration theories should directly and indirectly link migration flows to the direct involvement of the North in the South in order to present a more balanced view of certain migration dynamics (Lafleur and Stanek 2017b).

Due to the mistaken or exaggerated representation of the South as a place of chaos and need, the Eurocentric perspective does not see it – and, in particular, Africa – as having the social, economic and political conditions to attract migrants, especially those from the North. In conventional migration theory, the South is represented as sending migrants to the North in order to escape life's hardships (Castles and Miller 2009). This representation is reinforced by the ongoing images of migrants from Africa desperately attempting to reach Europe, migrants from Latin America at the Mexican border attempting to enter the USA and migrants from Asia in East Timor attempting to enter Australia by boat (Castles and Miller 2009). The question is not whether these images are 'true' or not but whether this is the only reality of the South. In the imaginative geographies of the North, these images represent the only or the predominant reality of the South and serve to present a homogenous discourse that perpetuates the view that the South can only be a source of problems.

The representation of the South as problematic and inferior serves as a means to control, dominate and make the South politically, economically and culturally dependent on the North (Power 2006). This representation is based on what Saïd (1978) called 'Orientalism', which is based on strong stereotypes about race, gender and social class.[6] Orientalism operates in a binary worldview of 'us versus them' and dismisses the notion that anything outside of the 'Northern' or 'Western' world could be considered of any benefit (Loomba 2005). So 'Orientalism' erased the history, culture and religion of the South and substituted it with the triumphant, redemptive and glorious history of the North. It destroyed the old and recreated a new identity linked with the North (Mudimbe 1988). The North becomes the point of reference and of departure of history and knowledge and, ultimately, a source of life and inspiration for the South (McLeod 2000). It is important to mention that there is, in this sense, an overlap between Orientalism and Eurocentrism; the difference lies in the fact that Orientalism operates more with reference to geographical distance and Eurocentrism operates across strong ideological differences.

2.4 Perspectives from the South: towards a critical understanding of asymmetries

As mentioned above, migration theories, whether directly or indirectly, are concerned with migration dynamics which primarily affect the North. However, that is not to say that these theories, dominated by Eurocentrism and Orientalism, are not at all useful but is, rather, an attempt to point out that they are insufficient to address some of the other and newer migration flows. There are other theories that try to critically engage and expose some of the dynamics and asymmetries at play in the relationship between North and South. One such theory that this thesis uses is the 'theory of the South',[7] which is concerned with understanding certain social and global phenomena from the perspective of the South (Comaroff and Comaroff 2012). It tends to problematise and disrupt paradigms that see the North as

---

6 This representation is essentialised to the extent that the entire group is defined by a single cultural identity and representation. Muslims have been represented as terrorists (Sayyid 2013) and black Africans have a long history of being represented as criminals, lazy and aggressive (Shohat and Stam 1994). These misrepresentations often turn into official policies, such as racial profiling (Sayyid 2013) and 'stop and search', which are common practices for identifying crime in parts of the North.

7 The concept of the 'theory of the South' used in this thesis is a general heuristic and catch-all category for approaches that deal with formerly colonised spaces. These approaches include theories such as dependency theory, orientalism, postcolonial theory and the coloniality of power.

the centre of the universe. Unlike Eurocentrism and Orientalism, the theory of the South is concerned with the asymmetry of power between North and South, based on long histories of colonialism, exploitation and intervention. It does so by drawing from critical historical analysis in order to see long-term patterns of colonial and postcolonial continuation and disruption. For the theory of the South, it is impossible to understand the region without including the historical and contemporary participation of the North (Comaroff and Comaroff 2012). In other words, the underdevelopment and chaos of the South are directly connected to the North's capitalist penetration. According to the theory of the South, the end of colonialism did not terminate the economic, cultural and political dominance of the North over the South (Latouche 1996; Wallerstein 1995). Indeed, in some cases, it strengthened the relationship between the former colonial masters, especially among the elites of the South (Bhabha and Comaroff 2002). Sen (1999) sees the North as dominating the South, not only economically and politically but also culturally. He writes:

> The contemporary world is dominated by the West, and even though the imperial authority of the erstwhile rulers of the world has declined, the dominance of the West remains as strong as ever, in some ways stronger than before, especially in cultural matters. The sun does not set on the empire of Coca-Cola or MTV (1999: 240).

The theory of the South is concerned with this dominance.[8] Sen's (1999) analysis is primarily concerned with the North's domination, in particular in areas where the South is expected to assimilate. This dominance is a one-way-street paradigm as it comes from top to bottom, from the powerful to the powerless (Latouche 1996). However, the theory of the South is not only reacting to the domination of the North but is also concerned with forming North-South partnerships based on mutual interest and respectability, rather than having one geographical entity dominating the other (Power 2006). It is concerned with the inherent hybridity of culture rather than with cultural, economic and political imperialism (Bhabha 1994).

---

8 Power and dominance are understood as having an ongoing influence on formerly colonised countries, how the past is structured and how international political and economic structures are presently dominating the South. For scholars like Escobar (1995), such domination and power are indicators of ongoing colonisation, as coercive power is used to impose economic and political will on weak and vulnerable nations. In this sense, the world is viewed, shaped and defined from the perspective of the powerful (Quijano 2010).

There are various theories of the South, of which the most important are probably dependency theory[9] and postcolonial theory. The main thrust of these theories is to deconstruct some of these asymmetries of power and expose their impact in the South (Mbembe 2001). According to such theories, the South is like a 'satellite state' – a state that is there to benefit the interests of the North and which can be controlled politically and economically by a superpower (Slater 2004). Slater is concerned mainly with the asymmetries between North and South America, in particular the impositions to the power of governments that are ideologically in line with the interests of North America at the expense of the democratic process in the South.

Theories of the South – and postcolonial theories in particular – can be useful in explaining many of the asymmetric North-South relationships between the colonised and the colonisers. These asymmetric relationships are viewed as a point of departure for the understanding of some of the social and global dynamics, including the production of knowledge.[10] The point of departure for 'Southern' theorists is from the perspective of those on the periphery, those who were once subjugated. This perspective can be extendible to those who have never experienced colonialism but are under constant dominance and subjugation, be they political, economic, cultural, religious or gender-related (Brydon 2013).

At the heart of the theory of the South is the notion that the reality of the South cannot be understood in isolation without continually engaging with the North. As such, history is not viewed as progressive or linear. Rather than pointing to fixed temporal and geographical periods and spaces, theories of the South draw attention to continuities, fluidity and interconnectedness (Abrahamsen 2003). They understand the present in the light of the past, while engaging with how the past can influence the

---

9 According to Slater (2004), dependency theory has different facets but its main thrust is the economic imbalance of power between the global North and the global South and how this imbalance leads to inequalities in the South. Thus, dependency theory is concerned with the historical exploitation of the global South through unfair economic arrangements, which benefit the global North and the small elite in the global South. This thesis is concerned with facets of dependency theory that deal with an imbalance of power based on the historical exploitation of colonialism. It emphasises the continuation of various forms of dependency in a postcolonial Angolan context.

10 Critique by the theory of the South is also used in order to challenge the dominant paradigm of producing knowledge, which does not take into consideration the experiences of those in the South because 'knowledge' is seen to be produced from a position of power and dominance (Grosfoguel 2010).

present from various perspectives and how the past becomes the tool with which to understand the reality of the present in the South. History is the key element to understanding asymmetries because asymmetries are rooted in the past.

The understating of migration from the perspective of theories of the South concentrates critically on the penetration of corporations of the North in the South, in particular in countries rich in natural resources. The dynamics of global politics are likewise key components in understanding migration dynamics both from North to South and from South to North (Massey, Arango, Hugo, Kouaouci, Pellegrino and Taylor 2006). This penetration is often based on former North-South colonial excursions, which established capitalist and dependency systems. In other words, there is a link between current and recent international migration and past colonial excursions, as well as the economic interest of global capitalist systems in the raw materials which the South is expected to provide (Massey *et al.* 2006).

I illustrate all of the above by highlighting some works on migration that have used theories of the South to understand particular migration dynamics, linking them to past colonial incursions. Interestingly, nearly all the authors I am about to cite in the rest of this section, as well as other 'Southern' theoreticians already cited (notably Slater 2004), are geographers, helping to link much of the conceptual and empirical research on migration, including my own, to the discipline of geography. First, Samers' (1997) study on Algerian migrants in France interconnects the past colonial penetration of France into Algeria as a cause of Algerian migration to France, in particular in the automobile industry. Samers critically engages with the past in order to understand some of the dynamics involved in Algerian migration to France by using postcolonial theory to highlight the links between this migration and French colonialism in Algeria. Although Samers' (1997) research is informative and critical, the work follows a typical South-North migration dynamic; the key difference is the usage of postcolonial theory and the role of the past in this migration.

Another work which uses theories of the South is the volume edited by Fechter and Walsh (2012). It uses postcolonial theory to understand how European migrants, in this case expatriates, enjoy certain privileges in the South. The volume is helpful to my research because it provides clear evidence of North-South migration and critically demonstrates the privileges that migrants from the North have in the South. It also uses postcolonial theory to conceptualise the importance of history in this trans-global migration trajectory. The point that Fechter and Walsh (2012) stress is linked to how European migrants in the South are treated differently. It is interesting to compare their (2012) volume and Samers' paper (1997). While Samers also concentrates on the exploitation and exclusion of Algerians in France, which is a typical South-North migration dynamic, Fechter and Walsh (2012) concentrate on North-South privilege, which is dominated by acceptance and the enjoyment of a luxurious lifestyle. Many of these dynamics are linked to what Massey (1993) refers to as 'power geometry', which is a reference to how various social groups and individuals experience the time-space compression of globalisation differently. According to Massey, people moving from a supposedly developed country to an underdeveloped country have a different experience of mobility because of the variable symbolic and real power of race, gender and class. In other words, spatiality and mobility are shaped by power differences; some people are able to move freely while others are much more limited. Different social groups and individuals have distinct relationships to mobility. 'Some are more in charge of it than others; some initiate flows of movement, others don't; some are more on the receiving end of it than others; some are effectively imprisoned by it' (Massey 1993: 59–69). The case of migrants moving from North to South reveals that they have significant power and privilege which, in turn, is related to the uneven geography of global power.

2.5 North to South migration: 'expats' and others

Given the geography of uneven development[11] between the North and the South, there is a difference in how migration from North to South is conceptualised. The literature on migration rarely theorises the dynamics of North-South migration, partly due to the perceived infrequency of this migration (Fechter and Walsh 2012). Lundström (2014) argues that the question is not so much about the infrequency of North-South migration or the conditions of the South but more on the terminology and implicit power relations used to describe North-South migration. Migrants from the North to the South are not considered to be 'immigrants', a term

---

11 The geography of uneven development in this thesis is concerned with the global division of labour between the global North and the global South. According to Harvey (2006), the global division of labour is partially a result of capitalism's penetration in the global South that has, historically, divided the world into a hierarchical order.

which somehow has a negative connotation in the current age of nativist and nationalist politics. Rather, North-South migrants are described as 'expatriates', often abbreviated to 'expats', which has a more positive connotation, somehow related to their high endowment of skills and wealth. In other words, North-South migration is connected to development and the transfer of skills, while South-North migration is viewed suspiciously. Collier (2013) considers South-North migration as detrimental to the development of the South, especially when it comes to 'brain drain'. He argues that qualified and skilled migrants in the South should stay in their home countries in order to help these countries to develop economically and socially. His logic is that there is a greater need for these individuals in the South than in the North. However, Collier's solution to 'brain drain' encourages authoritarianism because it requires a forceful restriction on the movement of skilled migrants from the South – which is a common practice of authoritarian regimes and which flouts the fundamental human right of a person to leave their country. It is interesting to note that Collier does not apply the same logic when it comes to North-South migration because he probably assumes North-South migration to be a skill or 'brain gain'. In other words, South to North migration is viewed as a brain drain and North to South migration as a brain gain for the South (de Haas 2008).[12]

---

12 Migration from South to North has also been dominated by a positive discourse of development (de Haas 2008) which tends to view migrants from the South to the North as promotors of development in the South through remittances. Migrants are also viewed as gaining work experience in the North, which is believed to be transferable upon return. There are many questions arising from the assumption that migrants automatically gain skills in the North (Piore 1979). Those researchers who assume that migrants automatically help to promote development in their country of origin forget to see that most migrants find themselves at the bottom of the economic ladder, face many obstacles such as redundancy and discrimination and hardly do any skilled jobs (Bauman 2004). As such, the question of 'brain gain' development needs to be carefully analysed, including remittances (Glick Schiller and Faist 2010). Positivist development arguments should be viewed with caution as should the impact of remittances and 'brain gain'; there is a neoliberal agenda beyond the exorbitant claims of development (Glick Schiller and Faist 2010). Piore (1979) points out that much of the remittance money is rarely used to promote tangible economic development that impacts on the infrastructure but it is used mainly for family consumption. Glick Schiller and Faist (2010) point out that neoliberals want to take away the economic responsibility of the state and give it to the migrants, whose remittances will then be the primary source of development in the South.

The differentiation between immigrants and expatriates is based not always on skills and professionalism but also on geography and race (Lundström 2014). The 'geography of race' plays an important role because the world is hierarchically divided; different countries are put in different categories and classes. These categories are also racialised and, as such, the experience of North-South migrants is not same as that of South-North migrants. As Lundström (2014) points out, the 'elephant in the room' is race and one can say that the term 'expatriates' is reserved exclusively for white Europeans and North Americans working in the South and does not apply to minorities in the North. The expatriate terminology carries with it connotations of power, privilege and class. Most of the studies tend to equate expatriates with professionalism, very high salaries, many additional 'perks' such as free housing and subsidised travel, high and specialised skills and short-term migration. However, Fechter and Walsh's (2012) study on expatriates is critical of the association of expatriates simplistically with skills or professionalism but, rather, explores issues of race, power and privilege. This view is also shared by White (2002), who argues that race is always a key component in understanding the dynamics of North-South encounters. To the extent that North-South migration is often associated with expats and high skills, the question of race and associated privilege seems to be ignored as insignificant. In spite of the suggestion by Fechter and Walsh (2012) and White (2002) to include race in conceptualising North-South migration dynamics, other writers such as Habti and Elo (2019) tend to concentrate on the skills and professionalism of expatriates and less attention is given to race.

2.6 Portuguese migration to Angola and the Lusophone migration system

In the light of the discussion above, the question arises as to where Portuguese migration to Angola fits within the North and South migration dynamics. One way of approaching an understanding of the Portuguese 'North-South' migration to Angola is via the theoretical notion of Portugal as a 'semi-peripheral' country within the global migration system (Arrighi 1985; Kritz, Zlotnik and Lim 1992). Early applications of the core–periphery model to Europe classified Portugal as part of the dependent periphery (Holland 1979; Seers 1979). This was not only on the basis of its obvious geographical distance from the economic and political heartland of Europe but also because of its role as a reservoir of migrant labour for the industries and construction sites of Northern Europe – particularly France,

Germany, Luxembourg and Switzerland. As Seers (1979) and, more recently, King (2015) have argued, migration is the most important functional link between the European periphery and the core, expressed in an asymmetric relation of power which reflects political economy, economic geography and social inequality. This relationship has a cyclical rhythm: migrant workers are drawn into the core from the periphery during times of economic expansion – such as the European industrial expansion era of the 1960s and early 1970s – and then blocked and expelled in times of recession, notably in the late 1970s and 1980s.

However, Portugal's migration dynamics are more complex than merely being a migrant-sending periphery in Europe. Portugal has also functioned as the metropole-core of a colonial migration system extending to Brazil and the (former) African colonies, based on its colonial history and the export of the Portuguese language and culture over many centuries. Baganha (2009: 8) called this the 'Lusophone migratory system', which is composed of seven countries – one fairly highly developed (Portugal), three of more-or-less medium development (Brazil, Angola, Cape Verde) and three with low development levels (São Tomé and Príncipe, Mozambique, Guinea-Bissau) – these development differentials being essential to the functioning of the system. Although some authors (e.g. Morier-Genoud and Cahen 2013) contest the notion of an 'autonomous Lusophone migratory space', I go with the majority view of Portuguese geographers and migration scholars that, at least at the descriptive level of migration flows and exchanges, the system 'exists' (Baganha 2009; Góis and Marques 2009; Malheiros 2005).

Today, Portugal maintains its Janus-faced position in the global migration system, looking both inwards to the core of Europe and outwards to South America and Africa –especially Brazil and Angola. Its multi-faceted and intermediate position within the global core–periphery hierarchy is precisely what qualifies it for semi-peripheral status. The defining characteristic of semi-peripheries is that they combine features of both central and peripheral countries, including the co-existence in space and time of immigration and emigration. Arguably Portugal's experience exemplifies this dual condition better than any other European country (King 2019).

However, as Góis and Marques (2009) convincingly show, the Lusophone migratory space does not have a single dominant core but consists of a 'tricephalous' structure in which Brazil and, latterly, Angola also act as nodes attracting inward migration. Thus, the Lusophone periphery is far from homogenous, not least in the way in which a fast-developing country like Angola draws migrants not only from the former colonial metropole but also from other countries both inside (Brazil) and outside (China, South Africa) the Lusophone system.

Portugal can thus be said to occupy an intermediate level in the global migration hierarchy, situated between the highly developed world of Europe (being on the whole a relatively poor country by West European standards) and the formerly colonised, still underdeveloped but increasingly heterogenous, 'Third World' (King 2019). It is both a sender and a receiver of significant migration flows. This also suggests, as Arrighi (1985: 45) confirms, that the semi-periphery is not an ephemeral or transitory part of the core–periphery system but, rather, a permanent, structural feature of it, albeit subject to changes over time.

2.7 Perspectives and myths: postcolonialism, coloniality, the work ethic and social capital

Despite Portugal's intermediate level in the global migration hierarchy, postcolonial theory would argue that Portugal's past was one of a colonial empire exercising significant power and privilege in its former colonies. Some former empires continue to influence their former colonies, in areas such as economics, politics and culture (Mbembe 2001; McEwan 2009). Postcolonial theory has been at the forefront in exposing and explaining how this colonial and colonised relationship operates. A particular emphasis has been put on the coalition of the elites in the South and governments of the North. The coalition has been critically exposed by postcolonialism as a betrayal of the principles of equality and freedom for the South. Critical scholars see the elites in the South as collaborators in the economic plight of the poor. As such, postcolonialism produces a continuation of the patterns of domination and exploitation perpetuated by neocolonial elites who, in some cases, culturally reflect former colonial regimes (Mignolo 2000). In this case, postcolonialists would argue that even a country like Portugal, with its moribund economy and its peripheral position within Europe, still has significant leverage on its former colonies – a leverage predominantly evident in what postcolonial thought has called 'mimicking' or the unreserved embrace of colonial cultural etiquette, values and myths by the elites of the South (Bhabha 1994).

One of the dominant social myths that separates the global North and South, which will be shown later to be particularly relevant to the case of Portuguese migrants in Angola, is the myth of the work ethic. The work ethic has been presented as a virtue and trait that is uniquely European

(Chang 2008) and is seen as being responsible for the high level of progress and development in Europe. This myth is not limited to the work ethic but extends also to intelligence (Herrnstein and Murray 1994). Harvey (2001) criticised Kantian geography for suggesting that both intellectual capacity and development depend on geographical location. People coming from tropical areas were considered culturally backward compared to those originating in relatively colder areas. Even though Kant's deterministic geography has been debunked as nonsensical, postcolonial theory has nevertheless demonstrated how this myth continues in subtle ways to dominate the relations between the North and the South (Shohat and Stam 1994). According to this myth, poverty in parts of the South is a problem not only of global economic structures that selectively pick winners and losers but also of geography, including climate and location, which allegedly discourages the work ethic (Shohat and Stam 1994).

Postcolonial countries struggling with underdevelopment have been characterised as having a 'work ethic' problem (Harrison 2000). For example, Etounga-Manguelle (2000) argues that the underdevelopment of the South is linked not so much to colonialism or any external forces but fundamentally to work ethics. The South and, in particular, Africa, needs 'culture adjustment' because of its lack of a work ethic.When he talks of culture adjustment, Etounga-Manguelle defends the failed policy of neoliberalism in the South and attributes it to the African culture and the continent's inability to assimilate the culture of the West. Etounga-Manguelle further argues in generalised and essentialised terms that, with the exception of South Africa, the rest of the African continent does not have the concept of a work ethic. This is the reason why economic schemes designed in the North tend not to succeed in the South. The problem, according to this view, is not that economic policies are a problem but, rather, that it is the incapacity of the people to embrace them because the requisite cultural norms are not present. As such, any economic policy in the South aimed at improving economic conditions should include some sort of training in the work ethic (Harrison 2000). According to Chang (2008), Etounga-Manguelle's (2000) views are not new and have also been used before to justify the supposed backwardness and inferiority of Japan and South Korea. These two countries used to be considered backward due to cultural and religious factors; however, once these countries became economically rich, similar to the countries in the North, South Korean and Japanese culture became a source of praise. As Chang (2008: 193) succinctly put it:

So, in the early days of capitalism, when most economically successful countries happened to be Protestant Christian, many people argued that Protestantism was uniquely suited to economic development. When Catholic France, Italy and Austria and southern Germany developed rapidly, particularly after the Second World War, Christianity, rather than Protestantism became the magic culture. Until Japan became rich, many people thought East Asia had not developed because of Confucianism. But when Japan succeeded, this thesis was revised to say that Japan was developing so fast because its unique form of Confucianism emphasized co-operation over individual edification, which the Chinese and Korean versions allegedly valued more highly. And when Hong Kong, Singapore, Taiwan and Korea also started doing well, so this judgment about the different varieties of Confucianism was forgotten. Indeed, Confucianism as a whole suddenly became the best culture for development because it emphasized hard work, saving, education and submission to authority.

The question is not whether the work ethic does play a role in certain instances but whether it can be understood outside of a long history of colonial domination or is, perhaps, a unique European trait. There are other dynamics at play that cannot be reduced to the work ethic. Alatas (1977) points out that the work ethic has been used to justify inhuman colonial practices in the past. It was used as a myth and discourse to put Europeans in positions of power and force so-called natives to engage in hard labour. Similar views are shared by Bender's (2004) work on Portuguese colonialism in Angola. According to him, the inhuman practices of Portuguese colonialism were often justified under the myth of the work ethic, which was assumed to be a unique Portuguese trait which could be imparted to Africans through slavery and forced labour under the rubric of civilisation. 'Civilisation' in this context meant forced labour to help the 'lazy native' to embrace a life of discipline and love for work (Alatas 1977; Jerónimo 2015). The work ethic is also used by the elites in the South as a discourse to protect their interests against those who did not make it up the economic ladder and who are thus to blame for not working hard enough or not taking seriously their personal responsibility.

The myth of the work ethic acts as a discourse to elevate the supposed superiority of a particular civilisation over the other and acts as a justification to explain the poor social conditions of most of the South, deliberately dismissing other possible explanations for the economic and political problems of the poorer countries of the world. The notion of the work ethic acts as a combination of geography, psychology and sociology but ignores history in its analysis. When history is acknowledged, it is analysed uncritically, more as the glorification of the achievements of the North (Ferguson 2012).

The work ethic can also operate under the umbrella of social capital. According to Bauder (2006), over the years most scholars have tended to look at issues of capital from a wide variety of perspectives. Adam Smith and Karl Marx viewed capital from a different perspective. 'Marx distinguishes between constant capital, which he associated with the means of production, and variable capital, by which he refers to labour' (Bauder 2006: 36). However, following but also refining Bourdieu's (1982) famous 'forms of capital' Bauder sees capital in different forms:

> Various form of capital are involved in the reproduction of society. Economic capital is a capital in its monetary form, as financial resources or fiscal assets. It is the most conventional perspective of capital and is privileged by orthodoxy over the other forms of capital. Social capital refers to social networks, membership in the social group, and social identity associated with membership. Cultural capital relates to physical behaviour, and organizational attributes of symbolic meaning and value. In the category of cultural capital, several subcategories can be distinguished; embodied cultural capital refers to corporeal appearance and performance; objective cultural capital refers to institutional diplomas, certificates, or other forms of institutional recognition (Bauder 2006: 36–37).

Social capital is a helpful tool for understanding some of the dynamics involved in workplaces and in various forms of employment (Portes 1998). However, an interesting observation about social capital is the absence of any mention of 'race'. True, there is a mention of 'physical appearance', which could mean different things but does not explicitly nominate race. In other words, social capital excludes one of the key factors in the analysis and explanation of social exclusion. According to Lundström (2014), race should be at the centre when analysing North-South social encounters or understanding the position of minorities in the North. She argues that the current global system is hierarchically and complexly divided on the basis of class, gender and race and that some groups and countries have certain privileges based on race. In other words, in some cases, social capital and the work ethic might not be enough, because of the overlooked factor of race. However, race is, in some other cases, explicitly associated with social capital and with the work ethic, which is understood as a unique characteristic of white Europeans. In this sense what Lundström (2014) is indirectly arguing for is the concept that Maldonado-Torres (2010: 97) calls 'coloniality'[13] and defines as follows:

> Coloniality is different from Colonialism. Colonialism denotes political and economic relations in which the sovereignty of a nation or a people rests on the power of another Nation which makes such a nation an empire. Coloniality, instead, refers to long-standing patterns of power that emerged as a result of colonialism, but that define cultural, labour, intersubjective relations, and knowledge production well beyond strict limits of colonial administration. Thus, Coloniality survives colonialism. It is maintained alive in books, in the criteria for academic performance, in cultural patterns, in common sense, in the self-image of peoples, in aspirations of self, and so many other aspects of our modern experience. In a way, as modern subjects we breathe Coloniality all the time and everyday.

Coloniality is a helpful theoretical notion because it captures in a single overarching concept postcolonialism, the myth of the work ethic, social capital and race. It shows that the impact and legacy of colonialism are forever present in the South. Colonial domination might not necessarily have a physical presence in most cases but it is present in different ways. The North sets the standard and criteria which the South follows. In these dynamics of a superior North versus the subordinate South, there is a greater continuation of dominance than of disruption. The South is captured by coloniality and there is, in this sense, a significant trust in the North. In other words coloniality is also about trust in the institutions and human capacity of the North. It is not surprising that, when it comes to migration, coloniality and trust play an important role and North-South migrants are treated as somehow exceptional. In other words, coloniality goes hand-in-hand with trust; trust in the capacity of North-South migrants to execute certain tasks based on where they come from. There is an interplay here between the past and the present, as postcolonial theorists would define it;

---

13 According to Bhambra (2014), coloniality is a concept that comes from South America and is concerned with colonialism events after, in particular, those aspects of colonialism that continue to dominate the colonised world following the logic of racial hierarchy. Given the nature of Portuguese colonialism in Angola, coloniality is a useful concept through which to understand some of the dynamics of Portuguese migration to Angola, especially the remnants of the Portuguese legacy. This thesis, however, does not deal directly with the question of decolonisation, which is more to do with a process of undoing and deconstructing aspects of colonialism that continue to dominate the world.

however, in this case coloniality sees the North's dominance as something that seamlessly and insidiously continues as the world battles with uneven development and the asymmetic geometries of power (Massey 1993).

2.8 Conclusion

This chapter has sought to demonstrate how North-to-South migration dynamics are dominated by asymmetric power relations which express themselves in multiple ways and are mostly inherited from the colonial era. The representation of the South as socio-economically inferior has given a sense that migration is happening only from South to North. The South is not only represented as inferior but is also viewed through the lens of Orientalism. As such, migration theories have payed less attention to the dynamics of North-to-South migration. In cases where such dynamics do occur, the discourse and conceptualisation tend to concentrate on the skills and privileges of Northern 'expats'. In fact, migrants from North to South are generally classified not as migrants but as expatriates, a term which refers not only to skilled migrants but also, indirectly, to 'white' European migrants. Expatriates are conceptualised differently to migrants from the global South who end up in the North – they are automatically thought of as privileged migrants. Therefore, North to South migration is not only about expatriates but also about the power that migrants of the North have in the South.

This chapter has also attempted to demonstrate the complexities of migration processes, looking especially at how global changes in the economics of production and in international relations have encouraged new forms of migration based on new divisions of labour in a postcolonial setting. Such changes require theories of migration that are less deterministic and normative. Moreover, they also require seeing migration not only from a Eurocentric perspective but also from the perspective of the South.

The theory of the South and its critical approach to North-South relations can be useful in mapping out and understanding new migratory routes and their associated constellations of power. As such, the South needs to be represented beyond the typical caricature of economic deprivation – as a place of destination for migrants and not just a sending place, as the Eurocentric migration paradigm indirectly assumes. Migration from North to South should be critically analysed from the perspective of colonial asymmetries which continue to play a significant role in parts of the South, notably through the concept of coloniality. The intersection of the present and the past is an important dimension in any understanding of North to South migration.

Chapter 3: Research methods

3.1 Introduction

This chapter presents an overview of the methods used to gather my research data on Portuguese migrants in Angola and on Angolans working with Portuguese migrants. It gives an overview of the challenges of doing research on North to South migration and presents the characteristics and background of the participants. I also address issues of positionality and reflexivity. Researching Portuguese migration to Angola is a complex task because it includes discourse analysis, the histories and legacies of colonialism, postcolonial culture and the global economic crisis, all of which shape the context in which this migration takes place and should be understood. One of the challenges which will be developed later is the question of precisely *who* should be considered Angolan and who should not, given the multiracial context of the country. The question of who should be considered as a Portuguese migrant and who should not is an equally challenging issue given the colonial history of migration to and return from Angola. Studies on Angola tend to ignore this particularity. The Portuguese colonial legacy continues to play a significant role in Angola and poses a challenge in terms of the criteria for who should be categorised as Portuguese and who should not. In order to overcome this impasse, my study employs racial categories such as Portuguese migrants, white Angolans, Angolans of mixed race and black Angolans. Precise definitions of these ethno-racial-national categories will be given in due course.

In order to comprehensively understand Portuguese migration to Angola, the thesis attempts to combine various methods, including semi-structured interviews, participant observation, discourse analysis, critical analysis of the Portuguese historical legacy and the study of postcolonial cultural dynamics. Two periods of ethnographic fieldwork were conducted, in Angola and in Portugal. The first concentrated on Lubango. Along with Luanda and Benguela, Lubango has been one of the preferred destinations for Portuguese migrants. The second part of the study was carried out in Lisbon, where my fieldwork was conducted because of the transnational nature of Portuguese migration to Angola. There are Portuguese migrants who are constantly moving back and forth from Portugal to Angola, depending on the economic performance of each country and conditional also on the migrants' visa status.

3.2 The challenge of researching North-South migration

Researching North to South migration can be challenging. One of the main challenges is finding literature that adequately deals with North-South migration. This kind of migration is not researched nearly as much as South-North movements and, even when it is conceptualised, it is done differently (Lundström 2014). Particularly lacking is literature on North-South migration in Africa. In order to overcome this impasse, I draw on literature used to analyse North-South migration in other parts of the world like Latin America, Asia and the Middle East. The works of Fechter and Walsh (2012), Hayes (2014), Hayes and Pérez-Gañán (2017), Lundström (2014) and Walsh (2018) are of significant help, in particular their use of postcolonial theory as a critique of some aspects of North-South migration. Although these studies focus on other continents, the patterns of privilege of 'Westerner' migrants are similar, though not identical, to those of Portuguese migrants in Angola.

Finding the literature is not the only challenge; another is how this migration should be conceptualised. Most of the voluminous literature that deals with South-North migration tends to conceptualise North-South migration as an exception to the rule, especially where sub-Saharan Africa is the destination. Åkesson's (2018) work on Portuguese migration to Angola is one of the few studies that does not directly conceptualise it in this exceptional way but attempts to approach this migration from different angles and on its own terms. Her work benefits significantly from her detailed fieldwork and particular insights but there are also differences between her research and mine. One difference is that, unlike her work, this thesis makes a sharp distinction between white Angolans and Portuguese migrants; it does not consider every white person in Angola as a Portuguese migrant, although it does acknowledge a link between white Angolans and Portuguese migration networks in some cases. My study uses a multiracial approach[14] and makes a clear distinction between white An-

---

14 The reference to the multiracial approach is an acknowledgment that Angola is a multiracial country composed of black Angolans, Angolans of mixed race and a small minority of white Angolans. In other words, in order to understand Portuguese migration to Angola, it is important to keep in mind the existence of

golans, black Angolans, Angolans of mixed race and Portuguese migrants. The second difference is that this study emphasises the historical connection of Angola to Portugal, in particular the legacy of Portuguese colonialism in areas such as language and cultural etiquette, as a factor enabling an understanding of some of the unique features of this migration. The thesis sees more continuation through the concept of coloniality than the disruption of Portuguese colonialism in Angola. Third, my fieldwork took place in Lubango, a different geographical location from Åkesson's (2018) research, which was conducted in the coastal cities of Luanda and Benguela.

There are two challenges that the Portuguese colonial legacy in Angola poses for this research. The first is the ongoing cultural legacy and the second the existence of complex family networks. According to Soares de Oliveira (2015), the Portuguese colonial legacy in Angola is very strong, in particular among the Angolan elite. This legacy includes aspects such as the acceptability of the Portuguese language and the associated indirect rejection of African languages, together with the mimicking of Portuguese norms and etiquette as signs of civilisation and progress. It is interesting to observe that a significant number of Angolans born after independence in 1975 do not speak any other language besides Portuguese. This anomaly is attributed to the nation-building process and the struggles by the Angolan postcolonial elite to create a myth of common descent (Hodges 2004). Moreover, the civil war also forced significant numbers of rural Angolans to migrate to the major urban centres like Luanda, which have a long history of strong Portuguese influence (Hodges 2004; Soares de Oliveira 2015).

As I showed in the previous chapter, the domination and elevation of the Portuguese language in postcolonial Angola comes directly from the Portuguese colonial system that treated the usage of African languages as a sign of backwardness and obscurantism (Bender 2004).[15] Under the colonial system, black Angolans were considered to be 'uncivilised' and were

---

white and mixed-race Angolans – in some cases, Portuguese migrants to Angola have ancestral links to generations of both white and mixed-race Angolans. Åkesson's (2018) work on Portuguese migration to Angola is valuable, although her distinction between white Angolans and Portuguese migrants seems less clear. This lack of clarity might indirectly confuse the association of white or mixed-race Angolans with Portuguese migrants and could alienate white and mixed-race Angolans – who do not see themselves as Portuguese migrants.

15 Bender (2004) pointed out that the Portuguese colonialists considered African languages to be detrimental to the civilisation process. Therefore, there was strong discouragement and stigma aimed at those who spoke African languages.

required to adapt through a process of assimilation which included, among many other things, gaining a command of the Portuguese language, reading and writing it and the ability to pay taxes and 'live like the Portuguese'. Once these requirements were fulfilled under the watchful eye of Portuguese inspectors, then a person could be considered 'civilised' and 'human' (Bender 2004). Ironically, both white and mixed-race Angolans were exempt from going through this process of 'civilisation' because they were considered to be assimilated by birth (Bender 2004). The classification between 'civilised' and 'uncivilised' Angolans set in motion a postcolonial society where these divisions became an embedded part of the society (Soares de Oliveira 2015).

Postcolonial liberation movements, above all the MPLA, were dominated by white, black (assimilates) and mixed-race Angolans (Mabeko-Tali 2018). The black Angolan members of the MPLA came predominantly from an urban ethnic group, the *Mbundu*.[16] The MPLA sought to present itself as a progressive modernist party which included all Angolans regardless of their ethnicity, race or religion and tried to paint an image of other political parties like UNITA and the FNLA (the National Front for the Liberation of Angola) as traditionalist, tribal and with no capacity to govern a diverse country like Angola (Mabeko-Tali 2018).[17] The FNLA was mainly dominated by the *Bakongo* ethnic group.[18] UNITA was dominated by the *Ovimbudu*.[19] Heywood (1989) pointed out that members of the MPLA belittled members of UNITA for their poor command of the Portuguese language and lack of sophistication. A similar critique could be made of members of the FNLA, who were considered to be uncivilised or not Angolan due to their being geographically and culturally closer to the Democratic Republic of Congo (DRC) and Congo Brazzaville (Mabeko-Tali 2018).

---

16 The *Mbundu* are the second largest ethnic group in Angola and are geographically located in the capital, Luanda, and provinces like Bengo, Malange, Cuanza-Norte and Cuanza-Sul. Henderson (1990) pointed out that the Mbundu are one of the most assimilated groups in Angola.

17 It is important to mention that this accusation that UNITA and the FNLA were tribal was part of the MPLA propaganda machine. In reality both organisations included all ethnic groups (Heywood 1989).

18 The *Bakongo* are the third-largest ethnic group in Angola and are located in the North of Angola in places like Zaire, Uige and Cabinda. Some of these regions border with countries like the DRC (Democratic Republic of Congo) and Congo Brazzaville.

19 The *Ovimbundu* are the largest ethnic group in Angola and are located both in the central region and along part of the coast, in places like Huambo, Bie and Benguela.

The denigration of UNITA and the FNLA as uncivilised opened the door for the post-independence MPLA government to continue to use the narrow Portuguese colonial definition of what it is to be Angolan. To be Angolan in postcolonial Angola was somehow associated with speaking Portuguese well, having a Portuguese name and having a myth of common descent – which is why one of the MPLA's slogans was *de Cabinda ao Cunene um so povo*, which loosely translates as 'from the most Northern part of Angola to the most Southern part, Angolans are one people'. This slogan in theory focuses on the myth of common descent and attempts to erase ethnic and racial differences. Ironically, before independence, the MPLA was engulfed with racial crises; black members of the MPLA complained that their leadership was dominated by white and mixed-race Angolans and these groups were accused of taking key positions of power and of not risking their lives in the war against colonialism (Mabeko-Tali 2018).

Perhaps the most interesting but also insidious aspect of postcolonial Angola is the continuation of the Portuguese colonial myth which presents Angola as a non-racial country with no problems of race and tribalism.[20] However, this borrowed colonial exclusionary definition of being Angolan does not take into account the fact that the Portuguese colonialists' assimilationist policies excluded the majority of Angolans (Bender 2004). Not every Angolan had the opportunity to be assimilated in the colonial system, which deliberately limited the education of black Angolans, resulting in only a relative few benefiting from education, with those who did being strongly associated with the Protestant Church (Bender 2004). Furthermore, the Portuguese colonial system tended to exclude rural areas and focus mainly on coastal ones. This ethnically and geographically exclusionary definition of having a strong connection to Portuguese colonialism has led some sectors of Angolan society to critically define Angola as *nação crioula*, literally translated as 'a nation of creoles'; however, in this context it means a nation of black assimilates (Soares de Oliveira 2015). The criticism is often directed at the urbanised black elites who were considered assimilated under Portuguese colonialism; these elites still

---

20 One of my participants, who was critical of the excessive Portuguese cultural influence in Angola, shared with me that his sister wanted to register her child with an African name and the government officer refused because the name was *too* African. There is historical evidence to support such claims. Under Portuguese colonialism, Angolans who went through a process of civilisation and assimilation were required in certain cases to change their names and take on Portuguese ones (Bender 2004).

mimic colonial cultural etiquette, feel contempt for African languages and culture and despise those who do not have a proper command of the Portuguese language (Soares de Oliveira 2015).

Most of the Angolan postcolonial elite come from the category of the *assimilados* (Soares de Oliveira 2015). *Assimilados* were black Angolans who were considered 'civilised' and who benefited from the exclusionary Portuguese colonial education system. They worked under the colonial system between the Portuguese colonialists and the so-called natives (Corrado 2008). In order to be considered an *assimilado*, black Angolans were required to reject the African culture, language, names and religions and to fully embrace Portuguese culture and civilisation (Bender 2004).

According to Soares de Oliveira (2015), the Angolan elite is more connected to Portugal than to the rest of the continent of Africa and some of the Angolan black elite also hold Portuguese citizenship and property in Portugal. It is not uncommon for those of the Angolan black elite to have strong Afro-pessimistic views and mistrust in the capacity of black Angolans. Soares de Oliveira's (2015) remark that there is significant admiration for Portugal by the Angolan elite is helpful in understanding the Angolan black elite and their connections to Portugal but does not go far enough to show that admiration for Portugal is not limited to them alone but also affects the general population. This admiration is connected to how the Portuguese colonial worldview was designed to see Angola and Africa in general as 'insignificant' and European metropoles as 'everything' (Bender 2004). Under Portuguese colonialism, it was common for Portuguese colonial leaders to boast about how much they have done for Angola in terms of building new cities and modernising the country and how Angola is different to other African countries. Portuguese colonialists also boasted about their capacity to live in harmony with black Angolans, which was not common in other colonies such as those of South Africa and Zimbabwe (Bender 2004).

While doing fieldwork in Lubango it became clear that, in order to fully understand Portuguese migration to Angola, it would be important to include white Angolans and their particular transnational family networks. Studies conducted on Angola tend to downplay the existence of other minority groups such as white Angolans and Angolans of mixed race. This is not just my observation but also that of Candeias *et al.* (2019), who seem to allude to the same findings. There are white and mixed-race Angolans who run businesses that are directly linked to current Portuguese migration to Angola. Some white Angolans were catalysts in helping relatives and friends struggling in Portugal to obtain employment in Angola. It is important to mention this because it is probably one of the particularities of Lubango, where a significant number of white Angolans constitute part of the upper class and control part of the private sector. The important element here is the correlation of Portuguese migration to Angola with family networks, something not happening for every Portuguese migrant in Lubango but certainly for a significant number.

3.3 Discourses framing Portuguese migration to Angola

Portuguese migration to Angola is dominated by different discourses and myths in both Angola and Portugal. During the time I spent with Portuguese migrants, I paid particular attention to the kind of discourse they use to explain their migration trajectory; I also analysed the dominant discourses mobilised in Lisbon during my fieldwork in the Portuguese capital. In order to analyse the discourses, I used Fairclough's (1992) method of discourse analysis, which is concerned with the written as well as the spoken word. According to him, discourse analysis is more than just hermeneutically analysing a text; it also includes informally hearing conversations and analysing the dominant collective narrative (Fairclough 1992). Discourse is also concerned with the analysis of a particular way of understating a social phenomenon (Jørgensen and Phillips 2002). In other words, it refers to the kinds of myth and worldview that are used to justify and dismiss a social phenomenon and to construct a homogeneous discourse of power in order to justify and normalise certain unjust practices (Torfing 1999). I analysed these discourses by socialising with Portuguese migrants and Angolans and carefully listening to their experiences and narratives.

My conversations and general socialisation with Portuguese migrants and Angolan participants took place mostly at their places of work, during break times and after working hours. Some conversations with certain participants happened more than once and I was able to clarify some of the points that were not clear. I also took written notes and made mental notes of every conversation after each meeting (Emerson, Fretz and Shaw 1995; O'Reilly 2005). As such, the discourse analysis drew on these conversations, which also included informal conversations related to migration in Angola and other general topics. Additionally, I used social media such as the Facebook page of Portuguese migrants in Angola and followed their postings to analyse some of the discursive patterns. The Portuguese migrants' social media are used as a network not only to organise work in Angola but also as a space for Portuguese migrants to share their more frustrating experiences of working in Angola, in particular the bureaucratic challenges. A similar strategy was also used to analyse the Angolan discourse about Portuguese migrants. Besides the social media discourse analyses, I also used online news articles on the topic of Portuguese migration to Angola as written from the Portuguese perspective and compared them with articles in Angolan newspapers on the same topic.

One of the dominant discourses, both in Angola and in Portugal, is that Portuguese migration to Angola is a skills-driven migration. Portuguese migrants rarely used the explanation that links their migration trajectory to the severe economic downturn of 2008 and subsequent unemployment crisis. They instead used a developmental discourse which focused on their contribution to the development of Angola, which consisted of two key elements: the first was skills and the second the work ethic of Portuguese migrants. According to some participants, Portuguese migration to Angola is helping the country to develop and modernise after years of civil war and destruction. Moreover, a closer look at the discourse on Portuguese migration to Angola echoes the colonial image of a backward Angola, an image which still plays a role in the everyday vocabulary of black, white and mixed-race Angolans and Portuguese migrants. It is not uncommon to hear words like *civilisado*[21] or *atrasado*[22] being used when things do not work well in Angola compared with 'civilised' Portugal. For many Portuguese migrants, Angola is still viewed as a backward country that needs to 'catch up' with the rest of the so-called 'First World'.

It is not uncommon for Portuguese migrants to invoke nostalgically the 'good old colonial days'; how Portuguese migrants' presence in Angola in the past would bring development and how Angola is benefiting again from this 'new' migration. Moreover, the developmental discourse is embroiled with the myth of the lazy native, often used in generalised terms to indicate that Angolans only want an easy life without working for it. It is important to mention that the discourse of the lazy native is used not only by Portuguese migrants but also by all parts of the Angolan population. This discourse does not acknowledge the pernicious structures that encourage inequalities or nepotism in the case of Angola but focuses on personal responsibility. There is an element of class in this discourse: black Angolans who think they have made it economically are quick to employ the discourse of the lazy native. Thus, in order to understand this discourse, I

---

21 *Civilisado* means civilised, someone who comes from an urban place.
22 *Atrasado* means backward, someone who comes from a rural place.

also use Portuguese colonial history to link some of these claims to Portuguese colonialism.

The literature on colonialism in Angola indicates that the discourse used by Portuguese migrants is rooted in Portuguese colonialism. It is not clear whether Portuguese migrants are fully or consciously aware of the colonial connections with some of the discourses used but the connections are stark. One could say, in terms of discourse, that there is more continuity with the colonial discourse than disruption. There is a dominant discourse in Angola which argues that things only work properly once a 'white' person is in charge or that having a white person as an employee is a sign of success. Empirical evidence for all the discursive frames and elements mentioned above will be presented in Chapters 4 and 5.

3.4 Arriving in the field

I chose Lubango as my preferred site for research firstly because studies conducted in Angola tend to overwhelmingly concentrate on Luanda. Moreover, as mentioned before, Åkesson (2018) had already conducted similar research in Luanda and Benguela. Lubango has also been a key destination for Portuguese migrants yet, as far as I know, no one has researched Portuguese migration to Angola in Lubango.[23]

---

23 During Portuguese colonialism, Bender (2004) conducted his fieldwork in Lubango.

Figure 1: Map of Angola showing Lubango

The city has an interesting history: under Portuguese colonialism, Lubango was one of the few cities that had a white and mixed-race population as a majority (Bender 2004), reflecting the strong history of Portuguese colonialism there. During the postcolonial era, the city continued to retain a significant white minority and mixed-raced population, generally doing better economically than the rest of the population living in a semi-segregated environment. The private sector in Lubango is still somewhat dominated by white and mixed-race Angolans, as are places of leisure like restaurants and shopping malls. The city of Lubango also boasts one of only three Portuguese-run schools in the country where the black Angolan elite, white Angolans and Angolans of mixed race send their children.

I arrived in Lubango in August 2015 and my fieldwork there lasted for two months. I had earlier lived in Lubango from 1995 to 1998 and had visited the city in between, although not for almost ten years. On my arrival in 2015, my first impression was that, in terms of infrastructure, there had been significant change and improvement, in particular with new roads, shopping malls, supermarkets and restaurants and a new airport. There was also chaotic traffic, which was not there when I left – an indication of the new economic prosperity – at least for some. There was also a visible increase in the white population, as could be seen in restaurants, banks and shopping malls. It was a clear indication to me that the place that I had not seen for nearly ten years was no longer the same – I felt like I was arriving in a new place dominated by changes. The same can be said about the people I knew in Lubango. Some of them had prospered economically, with stable incomes, expensive cars and thriving businesses. Yet some of those who apparently made it economically had become a bit more selective in choosing their friends, so the dynamics of class became more evident as well. However, while there was a marked change in infrastructure, there was also a visible continuation of old inequalities, as new infrastructures contrasted with old, living side by side.

I was surprised by how often I was mistaken for an outsider, especially when I went to restaurants dominated by Portuguese migrants and white/ mixed-race Angolans. Some Angolans assumed that I was a foreigner and resorted to communicating with me in English instead of Portuguese. In spite of these changes, I was still able to navigate the city, partly because I had a few contacts at the Protestant church which I used to attend. Some members of the church have worked with Portuguese migrants and one of the Portuguese migrant participants, ironically, also attended this church. Besides, before I left for fieldwork, I made the necessary arrangements in Angola in order to help with finding participants. One of the persons who promised to help me was a female white Angolan friend married to a Portuguese migrant. I had met this friend when I was studying in South Africa and she introduced me to other white Angolans.

Before the interviews were conducted in Lubango, I did a small pilot[24] study for two weeks, staying with my white Angolan friend. She gave me the preliminary information concerning certain group dynamics of Portuguese migrants in Lubango. She was also the first person to alert me to the existence of racist attitudes and discourses among Portuguese migrants and the difficulty of finding participants because these Portuguese migrants were not open to talking – especially to me, a black Angolan. In spite of her scepticism, she promised to find participants and show me the restaurants which Portuguese migrants normally visit. The Portuguese migrant husband of my white Angolan friend was reluctant to participate in the study or introduce me to other Portuguese migrants. He did not see himself as being like other Portuguese migrants but as someone who was contributing to Angolan development because he arrived before the economic crisis of 2008. In other words, some Portuguese migrants in Angola started arriving soon after the Angolan conflict ended in 2002. This shows

---

24 According to Bryman (2012), the pilot study is an important aspect of qualitative research because it indicates the feasibility of the research being pursued. Moreover, a pilot study helps to sharpen and adjust the questions of interest to the research.

the complexity of this migration. However, summarising, one can say that, although a small number of Portuguese migrants started coming after the end of the Angolan conflict, the main contingent arrived after the 2008 global economic crisis impacted on Portugal.

Although my white Angolan friend never really helped me to find participants, the two weeks that I stayed with her were informative because they enabled me to see other dynamics that I was not aware of, one of which was the connection between Portuguese migrants and white and mixed-race Angolans. In some cases these connections have played a significant role in the dynamics of Portuguese migration to Angola. It was through my white Angolan friend that I had the opportunity to meet other white Angolans and hear their views and discourses on Portuguese migration to Angola. White Angolans' relationship with black Angolans is at times based on class and self-interest. Black Angolans who are economically prosperous can easily intermingle with white Angolans. Moreover, intermarriage between white Angolans and Portuguese migrants is common, as is that between Portuguese migrants and Angolans of mixed race. However, intermarriage between Portuguese migrants and black Angolans is uncommon in Lubango. One of my Portuguese migrant participants is married to a black Angolan – they met at university in Lisbon and decided to migrate to Angola together, so their migratory profile is different to the norm.

My interaction with white Angolans and my general observations in and around the city helped me to see how race still subtly plays a role in postcolonial Angolan society, as well as the connection between Portuguese migration to Angola and white Angolans. The racism in the Angolan white community is not over but takes the form of subtle exclusion. For instance, I observed that some companies in Lubango are dominated by Portuguese migrants, white Angolans and Angolans of mixed race. When I asked a white Angolan manager why this was so, she responded by saying that there are not enough skilled black Angolans and that those who are skilled simply cannot do the job. On the other hand, interviewing skilled black Angolans indicated to me that the discourse of not having a big enough skilled workforce may be true in some cases but does not reflect other realities.

Before starting the fieldwork, I was not aware of some of the dynamics of race and power in Angola. Growing up, my experience with white Angolans had always been cordial, because some of them were reputed to have been involved in the struggle against Portuguese colonialism and some stayed in Angola during the civil war. However, the two weeks of staying at my white Angolan friend's place and socialising with her friends alerted me to the fact that race and class dominate the white Angolan community. I became aware that I was often the only black person at some of the gatherings where the other black Angolans were servants. I observed how exclusive the white Angolan community is in terms of marriage and places of leisure. I also became aware that it is impossible to understand Portuguese migration to Angola without looking at family networks. When I talked about my research with white Angolans, they were quick to associate Portuguese migration to Angola with skill and a good work ethic and contrasted these with the unskilled and supposed laziness of black Angolans, in particular those who had never left Angola. There was excessive trust in the capacity of Portuguese migrants, regardless of their ability; the fact that they came from Europe made a big difference. White Angolans also made a distinction between Angolans trained outside of Angola and those trained in-country – the former were treated differently and considered employable, whilst the latter were deemed unemployable. However, when it came to talking about differences in salaries between Angolans trained outside the country and Portuguese migrants, white Angolans were quick to point out that Portuguese migrants were 'expatriates'. Some of this information was gathered through informal interaction with white Angolans, some of whom held positions of leadership in companies that employ Portuguese migrants. I used the data from these informal conversations as part of my preliminary research.

Given the reluctance of my white Angolan friend and her Portuguese husband to help me to find Portuguese participants, I was compelled to change my research strategy from purposeful sampling to a more random and casual research design (Suri 2011). In other words, instead of depending on the contacts of my white Angolan friend, I decided to go around to business places, shopping malls, restaurants and bars to look for Portuguese migrants. Surprisingly, there was no resistance on the part of these latter, contrary to what my white Angolan friend had predicted. I am still not sure why she was reluctant to introduce me to them. She mentioned something about them being racist toward black Angolans but, in my experience, the racism was never personal towards me and only came in the form of a more general and implicit discourse when talking about work relationships with Angolans – and even then not overtly. On the contrary, most Portuguese migrants in Angola were cordial and friendly towards me. Chapters 4 and 5 will demonstrate empirically how racism operates among Portuguese migrants, in particular regarding the survival of colonial myths about black Angolans.

Although the more random sample approach was helpful in finding participants, it also proved to be problematic, in particular with white Angolans, who felt offended when I asked if they were Portuguese migrants or not. The lesson learned from this experience is that going around in Lubango asking every white person encountered if he or she is a Portuguese migrant can create issues. Thus, I resorted to snowballing as a secondary recruitment strategy, which improved the possibilities of expanding my field of participants (Bryman 2012). Once trust had been established, Portuguese migrants were willing to help me to find others. Moreover, they had a particular interest in my research because many saw it as a way to advocate for their plight[25] in Angola; they wanted me to tell the world how they are struggling with Angola's visa bureaucracy.

Whilst finding Portuguese participants was challenging at the beginning of the fieldwork, finding Angolan participants was relatively easy; most black Angolan participants wanted to share their experiences and frustrations of working with Portuguese migrants as well as their views on this migration. Once the interviews were conducted, black Angolans were eager to help to recruit more participants and so, here too, snowball sampling was used. Black Angolan participants were selected based on whether they had received their education in or outside of Angola. Their experience of working with Portuguese migrants was also one of the criteria for selection. White and mixed-race Angolan participants were selected based on their connection with Portuguese migrants. It is important to mention that I managed to formally interview only two white Angolans although I had the opportunity to interact with many others on different occasions, to speak about my research and to hear their responses. No direct interviews were conducted with mixed-race Angolans although I would point out that, at times, their identity and attitude were interchangeable with those of white Angolans. These two groups are interlinked in Lubango since, in many instances, they work in the same places, attend the same schools and have intermarried. I had the opportunity to interact with mixed-race Angolans when meeting in a group with white Angolans during the preliminary phase of the study.

The second part of the study was conducted in Portugal. The fieldwork in Lisbon started in July 2016 and lasted for six weeks. During my fieldwork in Angola, it was revealed to me that there is a back-and-forth

---

25 According to Sultana (2007), researchers working in the global South might be mistaken in being there in order to solve the needs and problems of the community being researched.

transnational dimension to Portuguese migration to Angola and that some migrants were only in Angola for a short period depending on their work assignment. This is one of the circumstances which makes the statistical estimation of the size of the Portuguese migrant population in Angola problematic. Moreover, this migration also depended on the relative economic performance of Angola and Portugal: when the Angolan economy is doing well, Portuguese migrants tend to stay longer and then, when the Angolan economy struggles, they tend to move back to Portugal. Another important perspective is the bureaucratic dimension. Due to the challenges, for Portuguese migrants, of obtaining a work permit, some worked for three months on a tourist visa and moved back to Portugal once the visa was about to expire, where they then applied again for another three-month visa. The fieldwork in Lisbon was meant to enable me to understand all these dynamics as well as the process of recruitment of Portuguese migrants to Angola. Thus, I attempted to look for Portuguese migrants who had worked in Angola and Portuguese companies that had investment partnerships there; I also noted the frequency of visa applications at the Angolan Embassy and looked at how Portuguese academics viewed Portuguese migration to Angola. Finally, I sought to understand the general public discourse on this migration. I made contacts via social media in order to find participants and some of my Portuguese migrant participants in Angola also helped me to find participants in Lisbon.

I had visited Lisbon before, in 2014, to attend a migration conference that focused on new Portuguese migration dynamics. During this period, I was interviewed by the German radio station *Deutsche Welle* in Portuguese. A second radio interview was conducted by the Blomberg journal in 2015.[26] What I found interesting about these interviews was that both discussions were dominated by the discourse that Portuguese migration to Angola is a skills-driven migration and that the Portuguese were going to Angola in order to rebuild and develop the country. The dominant assumption was that white Portuguese would only go to a country like Angola in order to 'help'. The emphasis was on the skills of the Portuguese migrants and on Portuguese construction companies in Angola. This discourse did make some sense given the postwar reconstruction process but

---

26 One of the journalists who interviewed me in 2015 was also a migrant in Angola and he helped me to find participants, directing me to Portuguese companies working in Angola. Ironically, this journalist worked for the former President of Angola's daughter and he was willing to share his experience of working with members of the political and economic elite.

it did not take into account the full complexities of Portuguese migration to Angola – namely the role of white and mixed-race Angolans in this migration dynamic – nor the relevance of the 2008 recession as a push factor.

Figure 2: Map of Portugal showing Lisbon

The media interviews and the questions posed by the journalists were helpful in understanding the dominant discourse around Portuguese migration to Angola. However, the fieldwork in Lisbon was challenging. Unlike Lubango, where Portuguese migrants could be found in specific places, in Lisbon they were very thinly spread across the city. Another problem was the constant cancellations by and unavailability of participants. Those who had returned and had secured jobs in Portugal were only available at the weekends because, during the week, they were often busy, whilst others simply kept on cancelling the meetings.

I repeatedly visited the two big construction companies in Lisbon with projects in Angola; however, they kept cancelling the interviews and recommending that I go to the head offices, which were located in Porto. The idea of visiting the construction companies was to see the strategies they use to recruit Portuguese migrants to work in Angola – there is a strong link between Portuguese migration to Lubango and the construction industry.

I visited the Angolan Consulate in Lisbon four times in order to obtain the cycle of visa applications between 2007 and 2016 and to try to understand why it was so difficult for Portuguese migrants to obtain visas to work in Angola. I also emailed the consulate a number of times without much success. Ironically, my colleague from the University of Lisbon, who was working on the same topic, managed to obtain the required information by simply calling and emailing the consulate. As for me, the information was not granted even though I repeatedly visited the Angolan Consulate in person. The response of the consulate showed how much power, race and privilege operate within the Angolan postcolonial state. European investigators working on Angola have, in some cases, greater opportunities to access certain information. There is a behavioural pattern of the Angolan state here: to present an image of openness to the outside world but, suspiciously, not to provide similar information to its own citizens.

A simple observation of other work conducted by European researchers in Angola enabled me to see how they were able to navigate with power-brokers and, in some cases, had information that was not available to Angolan citizens. The excellent work of Hatzky (2012) and Soares de Oliveira (2015) on Angola are good examples of this. In *Cubans in Angola: South-South Cooperation and Transfer of Knowledge, 1976–1991*, Hatzky (2012) shows how she managed to gain access to information that would be limited to anyone else in Angola. The same can be said of Soares de Oliveira (2015) who has admitted that, in Angola, there is an excessive trust in Europeans.

3.5 Research techniques: semi-structured interviews and participant observation

Doing research in Angola is not easy. Indeed, according to Schubert (2017) and Åkesson (2018), Angola is probably one of the most difficult countries in Africa in which to conduct research. Collecting 'good' interviews is a challenging task. Participants are often hesitant about having their views recorded. This attitude is partly due to the history of repressive colonial and postcolonial administration which resulted in the citizens living in a constant state of suspicion and fear. Recognising the difficulties of carrying out research in Angola, I designed a semi-structured interview schedule. According to Bryman (2012), semi-structured interviews are often helpful for teasing out some of the issues that could not otherwise be fully grasped through observation, focus-group discussion or study of the literature. Thus, in order to obtain and check the necessary information, I used triangulation and combined different methods (Berg 2004). To some extent, the semi-structured interview used in this thesis is the result of the insufficiency of other methods to provide the necessary information. However, even the interviews were quite challenging. Given the business of the participants, some questions were asked in follow-up conversations. In the case of Portuguese migration to Angola, a semi-structured interview was helpful because the participants generally wanted their story and their experience to be heard. At times, participants showed their unease at being recorded, preferring to freely express themselves only when the recorder was switched off. The participants in Portugal were free to say what they thought of their experience in Angola; only the Portuguese companies with investment interests in Angola refused to be interviewed. In order to fully grasp some of the dynamics, I carried out a follow-up interview with each participant once the recorder was switched off. During the follow-up questions and with the permission of the participants, I took written or mental notes of the conversations.

Conducting semi-structured interviews in Angola and Portugal was very demanding because most of the participants were often busy. Many of the interviews were conducted during working hours and breaks, when the time available was limited. In some cases, I met the same participant more than once in order to make sure that there was no discrepancy in the information provided. Once 'saturation' was reached, in terms of the consistency of the information gathered, I still continued to be in contact with my participants via social media and email. In other words, although some of the recorded interviews were quite short, the follow-up conversations tended to be longer and I include them as part of the semi-structured interviews.

In order to pilot-test my key research instrument, I tried out some of the questions in informal conversations with Portuguese migrants and white and black Angolans in Angola. This was done during the first two weeks of my fieldwork in Lubango. After the pilot study, there were some questions that had to be omitted and others reconstructed, given the emotional reaction they evoked. This was particularly the case with questions related to the salaries of the Portuguese migrants or concerning race. Some of the Portuguese migrants were quick to dismiss questions concerning racism, preferring to focus on skills instead, while some white Angolans spoke against Portuguese racist attitudes. However, both used a similar discourse of 'skilled Portuguese' migration and contrasted it with the 'lazy Angolans' discourse.

After the pilot study, I decided to conduct semi-structured interviews with Portuguese migrants, Angolans working with Portuguese migrants and white and mixed-race Angolans. The interviews were constructed according to topic and not in chronological order (Bryman 2012). The questions were asked according to the time and availability of the participants.

Some were open questions, put across in a conversational style. The questions sought to elicit the following information: where the migrants came from in Portugal, their educational background, the kind of work they were doing before migrating to Angola, whether the work they were doing in Angola was similar to what they were doing in Portugal, why they migrated to Angola, how they managed to gain employment in Angola and the nature of their work, whether they have family and relatives in Angola and, finally, their general social experiences in the country. I decided to opt for interviews with individual participants for several reasons. The first was in order to hear each participant's experiences in a context where they were free to express themselves individually. Secondly, it was difficult to organise several people into a group. Finally, there were different hierarchies among my participants and some might not necessarily have felt free to express their views in front of those who had a higher status. Doing individual semi-structured interviews also enabled me to 'control' various sample parameters such as an appropriate gender ratio and a range of different ages and racial groups etc.

I interviewed 22 Portuguese migrants in Lubango – 12 female and 10 male – whose ages ranged from their late 20s to their mid-50s. Some of the female participants migrated to Angola because they were married to white Angolans, while others migrated with their Portuguese partners and children; a further group migrated as single women and found their Portuguese partners in Angola. The prevalence of more female participants does not necessarily mean that this migration is female-dominated. It simply shows that there is diversity in this migration and that Portuguese migration to Angola is not male-dominated. Some male participants came to Angola with their partners, some arrived single and one was married to a black Angolan woman whom he met at university in Portugal, as noted earlier.

Most semi-structured interviews with Portuguese migrants in Lubango lasted 25 to 45 minutes, with unrecorded follow-up interviews lasting between one and three hours. These participants were often hesitant about voicing their opinion openly on tape but, once the recorder was off, it was easier to obtain further – and more frank – information. These interviews were conducted both during and after working hours and at weekends in bars, restaurants, cafés, universities, hotels and parks.

I also undertook participant observation, attending some lectures and classes at a private university in Lubango where Portuguese migrants were lecturing. I visited several businesses that employed or were run by Portuguese migrants and spent time 'hanging out' in spaces routinely frequented by Portuguese migrants, especially their leisure spaces.

This duo of research techniques – the semi-structured interview and participant observation – was also applied to Angolans. The Angolan participants totalled 13 and included those of different backgrounds who had direct experience of working with Portuguese migrants. The interviews also included white Angolans. The age range of the Angolans was similar to that of the Portuguese interviewees. In terms of gender diversity, the Angolan interview sample only included two female participants; an approximation of the gender ratio of skilled Angolans and business-owners. Besides semi-structured interviews and participant observation, I also made some general observations by visiting Angolan businesses that employed Portuguese migrants and observing the kinds of work that the Portuguese migrants were doing and the different discourses that Angolan companies used to justify their Portuguese migrant employment.

All the semi-structured interviews were conducted in Portuguese with exception of one that was in English. The interview questions were recorded and transcribed from Portuguese into English and manually coded. I did not used any software after transcribing all the interviews. I divided them into different topics and read them repeatedly in order to capture the emerging patterns.

The second part of the fieldwork was conducted in Lisbon, where 10 participants were interviewed. A survey questionnaire was designed and sent to a company involved in recruiting Portuguese migrants to Angola. This was done because the manager refused to be interviewed but, instead, offered to respond to and circulate the questions if I sent them via email. The participants included one female and five males. The other four interviews were reserved for Portuguese migration experts. The average age of my participants in Lisbon was early 30s to mid-50s. Most interviews were conducted in Portuguese with, again, the exception of one conducted in English. The structure of the interviews in Lisbon was similar to those in Angola, although some changes were made and more open-ended questions were asked. The questions for the migration experts were slightly different – the focus was more on explaining Portuguese migration dynamics and how the Portuguese migration to Angola is conceptualised.

Besides the methods mentioned above, I have also become an active observer and member of two Facebook groups, one dedicated to Portuguese migrants involved in (looking for) employment in Angola and the other dominated by white Angolans, in particular *retornados*. The Facebook page *Portugueses à Procura de Emprego em Angola* is dedicated to helping Portuguese migrants to find employment in Angola. The reason for using this group was to analyse the Portuguese migration discourse and the migrants' experiences and frustrations of working in Angola, as well as trying to understand the patterns of recruitment. Not many data came out of this exercise as the group became more interested in advertising businesses rather than providing a network for Portuguese migrants seeking to secure work in Angola.

The second Facebook group, *Fórum Kandando Angola*, was recommended to me by a Portuguese migrant. I befriended this group with the intention of recruiting Portuguese migrants for my research. However, the group was not composed of Portuguese migrants as suggested but, rather, was made up of white Angolans who had left Portugal after independence – those commonly known in Portugal as *retornados*. This group was also connected to white and mixed-race Angolans in Angola. The interesting aspect of this group was the network it produced which brought different people together and the subsequent platform it became for the 'remigration' discourse to Angola. However, the group was also dominated by nostalgic colonial discourses, in particular the notion of 'going back' to Angola in order to 'help'.

My observations and my participation in these groups did not bring anything that was new in particular but helped me, first, to understand the network of Portuguese migrants and, second, to grasp the 'skills-driven' discourse of Portuguese migrants going to Angola. The data collected though these Facebook conversations were not very different to those obtained through the interviews, so were useful for triangulation.

3.6 Characteristics of the participants

Having already outlined above the broad age range and gender characteristics of the interviewees, there are two main ones that this section concentrates on: skill and education. One of the dominant discourses of Portuguese migration to Angola is that of a skills-driven migration. It was therefore necessary to find not just Portuguese migrants doing these so-called skilled jobs but also those doing semi-skilled work, if this discourse was to be accepted or, more likely, challenged. Moreover, it was also important to find skilled Angolans, in order to get their perspective, too.

I purposely chose Angolan participants who had received a tertiary education, had obtained their qualifications either outside or inside Angola and had experience of working with Portuguese migrants. The criterion for selection was not necessarily to dispute the notion that Angola does not need Portuguese migration skills or that there are no Portuguese skilled migrants working in Angola. Rather, I am trying to understand some of the power dynamics at work in these relationships, given the long history of Portuguese colonialism and its legacy as well as ongoing myths. Therefore, Angolan participants are, typically, skilled individuals and include business-people, managers, university lecturers, government officials and consultants. They have first-hand knowledge of working with Portuguese migrants and acute perceptions of their skills. Some of the Angolan participants had studied in Portugal while others had studied in countries like Brazil, Cuba, Costa Rica, Namibia and South Africa. One of the participants was a government official who worked in the Department of Immigration and was responsible for handling visa issues for Portuguese migrants. Another participant worked as an advisor for the Governor of Lubango. One was a businessman who had a Portuguese migrant as manager of his construction company, while another used to be the leader of the opposition party in Lubango.

Portuguese migrant participants, on the other hand, were more randomly chosen, the only criterion being that they were, indeed, Portuguese migrants. Among them were private university lecturers, teachers at a Portuguese school in Lubango, a travel agency manager, a horse-riding instructor, a hotel manager, a hairdresser, a nail designer, a cashier and a salesperson. It is important to note that Portuguese migrants' skills and qualification are 'upgraded' once they arrive in Angola (Åkesson 2018). The jobs which some of the Portuguese participants do in Angola are not necessarily closely linked to the work they did in Portugal. For example, some of those who teach at a private university in Angola were not considered lecturers in Portugal because they did not have the necessary higher-level qualifications but it seems that they were upgraded once in Angola. There is excessive trust in the capacity of Portuguese migrants regardless of their actual skills, so coloniality plays a role in this artificial upgrading of their skills. More details on this general finding are provided in the empirical results chapters.

3.7 Positionality and reflexivity

According to Moss (2002), undertaking research in any context requires a person to be very conscious of issues of gender, race and class. My rather unusual personal history and positionality as a black Angolan doing my

PhD at a German university – and who has not lived in Angola for more than 20 years – might have influenced the way I carried out this research. It might also have influenced the way in which I have formulated the research and interview questions, the way I asked them and the way I engaged with the participants (Sultana 2007). I have tried to take this into consideration. Moreover, my unusual biography may well have influenced the way I was viewed by the different categories of my participants and other interlocutors.

For many Portuguese migrants, a black person doing a PhD at a German university was something special, because there is great admiration for Germany as a country among these migrants. Some wanted to speak about German cars or football teams like Bayern Munich. In other words, the global economic standing of Germany as a European superpower put me in privileged position and helped me to find participants. I was treated differently, as somehow 'civilised', not like 'other' black Angolans. I often had to affirm that I was actually Angolan and that I had spent part of my life in Angola, because some people thought that I grew up elsewhere. It was not uncommon for Portuguese migrants to make seemingly racist comments about other black Angolan colleagues but then to patronisingly say to me that I was different. My position as a PhD student from a German university did play a role in reaching participants – the outcome would probably have been very different had I been a PhD student at an Angolan university. I would probably not have been able to have access to the many Portuguese migrants in Lubango. Coming from Germany put me in a position of symbolic power, as Portuguese migrants assumed that I was different to the rest of the black Angolans. Some wanted me to report the difficulties they face in obtaining visas, which they saw as racism towards them.

My economic position as a researcher in Angola also played a significant role in the various ways in which Portuguese migrants and white and black Angolans perceived me. In Lubango some of the research was conducted in places like cafés and restaurants. In Angola these places are relatively expensive and, in Lubango, are mostly patronised by Portuguese migrants and white Angolans. The fact that I was able to visit these places put me in a privileged position. Furthermore, in some instances, I had to pay the bills of the participants. This seemed to put me a position of power and possibly influenced my engagement with Portuguese migrants. In Lubango, some cafés and restaurants are *exclusively* frequented by Portuguese migrants and white Angolans and it was not uncommon to be the only black person there, engaged in conversation with Portuguese migrants. It was also common for the waitress to assume that I was a foreigner and to try to communicate with me in English. In other words, a black person who can afford to go to spaces dominated mostly by Portuguese migrants and white Angolans is automatically assumed to be a foreigner or part of the small black assimilated Angolan economic elite.

In spite of this privilege, I remained aware of the fact that I was still a black person in the eyes of Portuguese migrants. My being black meant that I needed to find ways to negotiate conducting interviews with a privileged white group. I suppose that is why I chose to do individual interviews rather than trying to carry out research with focus groups. The individual interview was easier to set up and manage and to balance the associated power dynamics. Portuguese migrants were a bit reserved at first so, as a black researcher, I needed to find a strategy to gain their trust in order to interview some of them. One of the strategies was to present a letter from Bayreuth University stating that I was indeed a PhD student. Although the letter was written in English, the fact that it contained the university's logo was good enough to convince Portuguese migrants. There was also a participant who spoke German and had visited Germany as part of the Erasmus programme. She was a catalyst in mobilising other Portuguese participants for me.

The Angolan, particularly the black Angolan, participants treated me as someone who has made it in life. Certainly, there was this kind of imbalance of power between me and the black Angolans. Every time I introduced the topic of my research, I had the feeling that they looked at me as someone who would finally expose the ongoing discrimination which they face. They wanted me to advocate for equal payment for them and Portuguese migrants. I must admit that I do sympathise with some of the black Angolans and I am not neutral about the issue of the pay gap that justifies Angolans' low income just because they are Angolan. As someone who lived part of my life outside, I know what it means to be excluded based on how one looks. Given the imbalance of power between me and black Angolans, I needed to be careful not to come across as patronising or with an attitude of wanting to 'save' black Angolans from the apparent discrimination against them. Just as the Portuguese migrants wanted to me to spread the word to the world about their difficulties with visas, so black Angolan participants wanted me to broadcast the discrimination they suffer when it comes to salaries. All these dynamics might have affected how I formulated the questions, how I approached my participants and how I have interpreted my empirical findings.

When encountering white Angolan participants, the power dynamics were a bit different. It somehow felt more like doing an elite interview or observing an elite group. The first observation was the fact that I was often the only black person during social events. Second, I do not come from a typical rich black Angola family, so I was a bit of an enigma to the white Angolans. As such, they wanted to know more about my background. In such cases my positionality as a PhD candidate did not necessarily help. Once some white Angolans found out that I was not part of the political and economic elite, they did not know how to interact with me. It was strange for them that someone who does not belong to a particular class could do something which, in Angola, is indirectly reserved for the chosen few. The class aspect in combination with race was important. Oftentimes, I had to assert myself with the white Angolans who participated in this research since they were not, on the whole, a vulnerable group. I might have been biased in observing some of the dynamics. I was particularly critical of the anti-colonial discourse foregrounded by white Angolans while, at same time, operating in semi-segregated enclaves where relationships with black Angolans are those of masters and subordinates. Some of these social dynamics might be purely class-related but, in many cases, race and class in Angola go together. Even though, for some of the white Angolans who have been in Angola for four or five generations, their interaction with me as a black Angolan was different, there is a certain historical privilege attached to being white in Angola. At times, I felt more welcome when it came to engaging in conversations about the current political situation in Angola. At others, I was on the margins, especially when it came to the questions I put to white Angolans about their experiences of working with black Angolans. Challenging the use of colonial discourses of the lazy native while boasting about the credentials of being anti-colonial was not always welcome.

The gender element also played a role in my interaction and interviews with female participants. I am male, heterosexual and married with children. I cannot pretend that these characteristics might not influence my interpretation of and interactions with female participants and, in turn, have implications on the way in which I perceived certain gendered realities. Some of the Portuguese female migrant participants were married, had partners or were divorced and were single mothers. I had to grapple with the fact that, in spite of the relative privileges that Portuguese women have in Lubango in comparison with Angolan women, they are also humans who were pushed to migrate to Lubango by the cyclical vicissitudes of the often-brutal global capitalist system. There were moments of empathy as well as moments of critical reflection on some of the things they said. A moment of empathy emerged at the point when participants said they sent some of their remittances to help family members in Portugal. The condescending nature of how some female Portuguese migrants spoke about going to Angola in order to help poor children, when their migration trajectory to Angola was linked to the economic crisis, was something that left me surprised. There was always a sense that they were coming from Europe in order to help. Regarding Angolan female participants, the dynamics were relatively different; even though they were skilled, their struggles remained unlike those of Portuguese migrants. I needed to be more sensitive in formulating and asking certain questions in order not to be misunderstood, as issues concerning income, marital status and children are contextually very sensitive in Angola.

While the research in Lubango was informed by my positionality as a black male PhD candidate at a German university, this never had the same implications in Lisbon. My positionality as a relatively privileged black person was not as important. My Lisbon fieldwork felt more like my encounter with white Angolans in Angola.

On my way to fieldwork in Lisbon, by sheer coincidence I met an ex-Portuguese migrant in Angola at Nuremberg airport. She shared with me that her family were migrants in Luanda for two years but that, now, her husband had relocated to Erlangen and was working for Siemens. At first she was relatively keen to help me to find more participants in Lisbon and spoke of knowing 15 families who had worked in Angola and have since returned to Lisbon. However, she became highly suspicious about me and started asking personal questions. How did I get to Germany? How long had I lived in Germany? What was I doing before going to Germany? What would I be doing after completing my PhD? Would I stay in Germany or go back to Angola? Although she gave me her contact details and promised to help me to find more participants, she never answered my calls. In a similar fashion, some returned Portuguese migrants in Lisbon responded positively when I contacted them in English but cancelled when they realised that I was an Angolan PhD candidate at a German university. Fikes (2009) argues that the relationship between African migrants and the Portuguese in Lisbon is that of servant and master. There are certain spaces where African migrants are not expected to be; there are certain invisible boundaries. I should be the one being interviewed, not the one doing the interviewing; I should be the object of the research, not the researcher asking questions. In researching Portuguese migrants in Angola I was, in a sense, inverting the order of things. One Portuguese participant patronisingly told me that I needed to go back to Angola once I had completed my studies because Angola needs skilled people like me and that Portugal cannot continue to supply skilled workers to help the development of Angola. It is not surprising that some Portuguese migrants in Angola were keen to share their migration experiences, in particular their problems with visas but, once in Portugal, the situation changed.

Thus, my positionality varied from context to context: in some cases I was the privileged one, in others I was just another black Angolan taking chances. All these experiences and shifting positionalities have shaped my understanding and interpretation of some of the dynamics of Portuguese migration to Angola.

3.8 Conclusion

This chapter has described and accounted for the methods used to gather the information for my thesis. In order to understand Portuguese migration to Angola, it is necessary to adopt different methodological approaches. Some of the methods chosen, like individual interviews rather than focus groups, were selected in order to be sensitive to the context. Portuguese migration to Angola is complex and surrounded by different discourses and myths. The methods used in this thesis have helped me to see how Portuguese migration to Angola has emerged as a consequence of various intersections – many of them associated with the colonial legacy – which include family networks and colonial cultural influences. Through conducting semi-structured interviews, together with participant observation, I was able to grasp the major issues and dynamics at work in this migration process. Next, Chapter 4 will empirically demonstrate how the data gathered using these methods will facilitate our understanding of Portuguese migration to Angola.

Chapter 4: The legacy of the myth of Lusotropicalism in Angola

4.1 Introduction

This chapter argues that Portuguese migration to Angola needs to be understood within the history and legacy of the broad colonial notion known as Lusotropicalism. Lusotropicalism is actually composed of various myths, one of which was that of a non-racist and benevolent Portuguese colonial system (Bender 2004). According to this myth, Portuguese colonialism was exceptional because the Portuguese had the capacity to be non-racist and adapt to the so-called native culture (de Sousa Santos 2002). Lusotropicalism promotes the view that the geographical location of Portugal as a Southern European country, with its warmer climate and historical multicultural background, has predisposed its society to be open and receptive to other cultures and races (Freyre 1946). Despite the persistent dismissal of Lusotropicalism as a myth, scholars such as Cahen (2012) indicate that some tenets of Lusotropicalism still continue to dominate the imaginary of the Portuguese national identity as a non-racial society. In Portugal, Lustropicalism cuts across ideological divides. Many Portuguese still believe in its basic principles, including those who opposed Portuguese colonialism (Bender 2004). Lusotropicalism is not only embraced in Portugal, it is also held to in postcolonial Angola, in particular the myths of a non-racial society and common descent. The main focus of this chapter is the Portuguese legacy in Angola and Lusotropicalism as one of the umbrella notions of this legacy. The chapter looks at selected historical episodes of Lusotropicalism by tracing its origins in Brazil and its transition to Portugal and then to the colonies. The chapter combines histories of Lusotropicalism with empirical data on its legacy in Angola in the form of interview extracts and ethnographic observations. I particularly emphasise race relations among Angolans and how this relates to recent Portuguese migration to Angola.

4.2 The roots of Lusotropicalism

The roots of Lusotropicalism can be traced through the work of Brazilian sociologist and anthropologist Gilberto Freyre (1900–1987). According to Bender (2004), Gilberto Freyre was born in Recife, in Brazil, studied in the USA and is commonly known as the 'father' of Lusotropicalism. Castelo (1998) credits Freyre as one of the founders of multicultural studies, even though Freyre never used the word multiculturalism. Freyre's ideas of Lusotropicalism were first applied within the Brazilian context and are based on his own experience of Brazilian race relations in comparison to what he experienced in the USA in the 1930s (Bender 2004). Lusotropicalism emerged at a time when racial superiority theories were developing in Europe, the USA, Australia and South Africa – when the world was dominated by a worldview of racial hierarchies that regarded white Northern Europeans as the epicentre of human evolution and civilisation (Bender 2004). Needless to say, all other groups were considered to be inferior, uncivilised and even sub-human and subjected to rule and dominance by white Europeans (Bender 2004). One of the main questions was how the so-called 'superior race' should relate to inferior races. Some countries like the USA and South Africa embarked on racial segregation, policies that discouraged racial mixings because they were deemed as disobedience to God's hierarchical order (Bender 2004). Against this background, Gilberto Freyre did something that was considered revolutionary for the time. Instead of viewing racial mixing as a degeneration of the so-called 'superior race', he drew from his personal experience of Recife and Brazil as a case study that showed that racial hybridity was not necessarily bad. He presented a romanticised case of racial relations in Brazil that was devoid of the tension and segregation that the USA succumbed to. Freyre saw racial mixing as a strength and as something that should be celebrated and embraced. In a world dominated by racial tension and theories of racial purity, Freyre deconstructed the myth of racial separation and presented a case where different groups interacted with one another without visible racial barriers (Freyre 1946). Therefore, it is not far-fetched to attribute to Freyre's work the origins of current studies on diversity and hybridity (Castelo 1998) and, more specifically, our understanding of Portuguese–Angolan migration and race-relations dynamics.

In his popular book *The Masters and the Slaves: A Study in the Development of Brazilian Civilization*, Freyre (1946) credited Portuguese colonialism in Brazil as the key component of creating a society devoid of racial tensions, where different groups could live amicably together. Freyre defined Portuguese colonialism as being colour-blind and constructed the Portuguese male as not having problems being in a romantic relationship with a black or an Indian woman.[27] Freyre (1946) concluded that white Brazilians' amicable relationships with Afro-Brazilians and Indians were a result of Portuguese colonial exceptionalism. According to him, Portuguese colonial policy did not encourage the separation of races but their blending. The Portuguese propensity to hybridity was due to Portugal's geographical location – in particular, its warm Mediterranean climate which allowed Portuguese colonialists to be open to other cultures. In other words, Freyre associated the Portuguese geographical location with Portuguese culture, thus linking nature and culture to the behaviour of hybridity.

Freyre's ideas of racial hybridity and the inclusion of Afro-Brazilians and Indians as part of the Brazilian nation were first rejected by the Brazilian elite because the country was still hypocritically defined as one of European rule and Afro-Brazilians and Indians as somehow sub-human (Bender 2004). However, Freyre's ideas were later accepted and adopted as part of the national culture as Brazil redefined itself as a country also composed of African and Indian elements (Bender 2004), whose inclusion as part of the Brazilian national fabric was a significant step towards the representation of the country as one of diversity and racial inclusion, in contrast to the USA and South Africa and their stark segregation laws (Twine 2000). Freyre's ideas became so embedded in Brazil's national identity that the country was viewed by the outside world as an exemplary society when it came to racial diversity. Some, like Twine (2000), even considered Brazil to be a country without racism; he further points out that many African-Americans naïvely viewed Brazil as an ideal example of a 'non-racial' society with no history of lynching, no 'Jim Crow' ideology and none of the racial riots and protests which were and still are part of American race relations.

Although Brazil did not have the racial tensions of the USA and South Africa, Freyre's Lusotropicalism was questioned and critiqued as a myth (Bender 2004). Most criticism stemmed from the fact that, whilst Brazil

---

27 Krug (2011) criticised Freyre's work because of the hyper-sexualisation of black and mixed-race women. He argues that Freyre's Lusotropicalism concentrates on the relationship between white men and black women but does not say much about black men's relationships with white women. According to Krug, white men's and black women's relationships in Freyre's work were dominated by highly gendered power dynamics.

had the biggest black population outside of Africa, the upward social mobility of Afro-Brazilians was much slower in comparison to countries like the USA with its history of stark racial segregation (Twine 2000). Afro-Brazilians were under-represented in education and professional jobs and were reduced to doing manual jobs. There were invisible structures that limited the economic progress of Afro-Brazilians (Twine 2000). Freyre's argument failed to see those structures of exclusion and other forms of racial discrimination in Brazil and reduced the complex interactions between white Brazilians and Afro-Brazilians and Indians to cordiality. Freyre's response to some of the criticism was to point out that Brazil did not have a race problem but a class problem. In other words, the system of exclusion of Afro-Brazilians was not racist but economic. Much of Freyre's position stems from the view that Brazil did not have official segregation laws or the prohibition of interracial marriage (Twine 2000). Thus class, not race, was the main problem in Brazil, according to Lusotropicalism. Despite Freyre's idealistic 'non-racial' views of Brazilian society, the Portuguese colonial regime adopted some of his ideas of Lusotropicalism as part of its colonial reality, in particular the notion that the Portuguese colonial system was exceptional because the colonisers also lived in harmony with the colonised, devoid of racial tensions, in other Portuguese colonies as well.

4.3 The Portuguese colonial adoption of Lusotropicalism

Lusotropicalism was first rejected by the Portuguese colonial regime of the *Estado Novo* (Castelo 1998). At the heart of this rejection was the assumption made by Freyre that the Portuguese were predisposed to racial mixing because of Portugal's geography as well as the historical influence of the Arabs and Jews (Bender 2004). Such ideas of racial hybridity went against the colonial regime's position, which still subscribed to the dominant European worldview that saw racial mixing as negative, especially when it involved white Europeans with black Africans. Moreover, the colonial regime rejected Lusotropicalism in Africa because it still considered black Africans as inferior, uncivilised savages. Bender (2004) points out that some members of the colonial regime even believed that it was a waste of time and resources to try to civilise black Africans because they were beyond the possibility of being civilised. In other words, Lusotropicalism's notion of the Portuguese natural predisposition to cohabit with 'uncivilised' black Africans was too much for the colonial regime to accept. This was mainly because the Portuguese colonial system still upheld some form of white supremacist ideology (Jerónimo 2015). However, the anti-Lusotropicalism sentiment of the Portuguese regime softened when countries like England and France started relinquishing their colonies after the end of the Second World War (Bender 2004). This put significant pressure on the Portuguese colonial regime, as it was not ready to release its colonies but, rather, was determined to keep them. In the face of mounting criticism, the Portuguese colonial regime shifted its position on Lusotropicalism to embrace it as an official Portuguese colonial policy, with an emphasis on the myth of a non-racial Portuguese colonial system and racial hybridity as unique characters (Castelo 1998). Freyre saw Lusotropicalism as a sociological phenomenon but the Portuguese colonial regime adopted it as a political ideology and used it as propaganda to help keep its colonies (Bender 2004).

4.4 Lusotropicalism as a colonial propaganda ideology

In order to spread the ideology of Lusotropicalism, the colonial regime invested significantly in propaganda. According to Castelo (1998), schools and universities in both Portugal and the colonies were encouraged to promote Lusotropicalism as an exceptional trait of the Portuguese colonial system. Portugal was presented as this great civilisational power that opened up the world to Europe with a unique calling to civilise the backward native in the colonies (Bender 2004; Jerónimo 2015). The propaganda was not only aimed at spreading the myth of Lusotropicalism in Portugal but also intended to make this myth known internationally. The international campaign focused on the exceptional capacity of the Portuguese to live in harmony with Africans in the colonies as well as emphasising the benefits that the Portuguese colonial system brought to them. One of the benefits was the assimilation of Africans to the Portuguese way of life and the introduction of the Christian faith (Bender 2004). At a time when social Darwinism dominated Western thought, Lusotropicalism was presented as an example of how the Portuguese colonial system could transform black Africans from backwardness into civilised people and from 'sub-human' into 'full-human' (Castelo 1998; Jerónimo 2015).

The propaganda also spread in the domain of sport. For instance, just as in Brazil, where one of the greatest sports figures was the black footballer Edson Arantes do Nascimento, or 'Pele', so Portuguese colonialists in Africa groomed a mixed-race footballer called Eusébio da Silva Ferreira, internationally known as 'Eusébio'. He became an international symbol of the Portuguese non-racial colonial system. The interesting thing about Eusébio was that he was born in Mozambique from a relationship between a white settler from Angola and a black Mozambican woman (Serrado 2012). Such a relationship concretised the image of what Lusotropicalism preached. Eusébio was presented as a symbol of the Portuguese non-racial colonial system and was celebrated as the king of Portuguese football.[28] The logic of such propaganda was that, if Eusébio, as a mixed-race person from an African colony, could be accepted as a national hero at a time when apartheid was accepted by most of Northern Europe, then the Portuguese colonial system was indeed exceptional and should be allowed to continue in Africa (Bender 2004).

The colonial regime did not only involve popular sporting figures like Eusébio but also involved the participation of intellectuals like the founder of Lusotropicalism, Gilberto Freyre (Castelo 1998). Freyre was invited by the Portuguese colonial regime to tour the colonies in Africa in order to show how Lusotropicalism had been operating in other Portuguese colonies. After this period of touring, Freyre (1961) wrote the book *The Portuguese and the Tropics* and confirmed some of his thesis in his previous work on Brazilian Lusotropicalism. Freyre again praised the Portuguese mode of colonialism, in particular with the 'civilisation' of the 'native', the evidence of mixed-race families and an allegedly non-racial colonial system (Freyre 1961). Ironically, as in Brazil, Freyre's visit to the Portuguese colonies in Africa and Asia ignored the power dynamics of coloniser and colonised. He overlooked the subservient position of the colonised and superficially observed the supposedly amicable relations between coloniser and colonised without looking at the oppressive structures that maintained the colonised in a subservient position. Once again, he concluded that Portuguese colonialism was exceptional, benevolent, amicable and non-racial (Castelo 1998); an example to other models of colonialism such as those in Zimbabwe and South Africa. The Portuguese colonies had no segregated schools or public spaces and the colonised were regarded as fully assimilating into Portuguese culture, language and Christianity (Freyre 1961). The underlying argument of Freyre's Lusotropicalism and of the Portuguese colonial presence in Africa and Asia was the notion that Portuguese colonialism dispensed goodness to helpless natives. As such, the Portuguese

---

28 It is important to mention that Pele and Eusébio were outstanding sportsmen for Brazil and Portugal respectively and their success was primarily due to their extraordinary football talent; however, it should also be noted that their success was made to symbolise a myth of non-racial societies.

should be allowed to stay longer in order to complete the development process of Africa. In so doing, Freyre ignored some of the atrocities committed during the Portuguese colonial system under the myth of trying to bring the so-called native into Portuguese civilisation. Freyre also downplayed the existence of racism and the economic plight of the majority of Africans at the expense of an imagined unity and harmony which did not exist in reality.

As scholars like Bender (2004) point out, there was a clear discrepancy between what Freyre claimed about Lusotropicalism and what was actually happening in the Portuguese colonies, in particular in Angola. Although Portuguese colonialism did not have laws such as those of apartheid, there were other social mechanisms available to exclude black Africans from fully exercising their citizenship rights (Bender 2004). The Portuguese colonial system was hierarchical and divided different racial groups without having any official racist laws. It was a system that operated like an invisible wall – each group knew where it stood socially and economically within the racial hierarchy of the Portuguese colonial system. Whites were seen as being on top, then those of mixed race, then the black assimilates until finally, at the bottom, came the rest. Public spaces like restaurants and parks in urban areas were reserved for certain groups without the explicit signs that were erected in South Africa under the apartheid regime (Bender 2004). Therefore, Lusotropicalism was a propaganda that avoided the need to deal with racially stratified colonies and promoted a mythical unity which, in reality, was not there. The primary motive to embrace Lusotropicalism by the Portuguese colonial regime was to keep the colonies, even if that meant the implementation of cosmetic economic reforms, as the next section demonstrates.

4.5 Lusotropicalism and colonial reforms

Lusotropicalist propaganda not only involved representing an amicable relationship between coloniser and colonised but also included reforms aimed at winning the sympathy of a critical international community as well as dissatisfied Angolans and other colonial residents (Bender 2004). The first step to convince the international community was an attempt to recast Portuguese colonies as provinces of Portugal or *Províncias ultramarinas* – overseas provinces. This strategy broke away from a long-standing colonial position that defined the colonies as part of the Portuguese empire. The new position sought to 'integrate' the colonies into Portugal by erasing geographical and cultural differences between Portugal and the colonies and unifying all under one rule (Castelo 1998). In other words, according to the Portuguese colonial regime, Angola, Mozambique, Guinea-Bissau, São Tomé and Príncipe and Cape Verde were considered as provinces of Portugal, which was therefore presented as being bigger than Germany, France and England (Almeida and Corkill 2015). Although the new colonial reform emphasised the integration of the colonies as part of Portugal, the underlying motive was to project an image of the benevolent nature of the Portuguese colonial system which had the capacity to consider inferior African countries as equal parts of a superior European metropole. It was an attempt to erase differences and unify the colonies under a single cultural identity; that of 'Portuguese' (Bender 2004). This reform in theory considered everyone to be a Portuguese citizen regardless of colour; the only requirement was to embrace Portuguese civilisation.

Portuguese colonial reform not only recognised the colonies as provinces of Portugal but also included economic reforms such as the construction of new cities, towns and roads, the abolition of oppressive laws like forced labour recruitment and the elimination of assimilation laws which hierarchically divided black Angolans according to their assimilation status within the colonial caste-like system (Bender 2004). Some black Angolans who experienced and benefited from economic reforms look back at this colonial period with great fondness, especially when they compared it with postcolonial material deprivation and civil war (Åkesson 2018). During my fieldwork in Lubango it was not uncommon to meet an elderly person with fond memories of the Portuguese colonial system during the 1960s and early 1970s, as exemplified by this nostalgic quote: *'During colonial times we had jobs, salaries were paid on time, but today we do not even have water or electricity and the salaries are always late'* (Pedro, August 2015). However, Pedro did not seem to remember that the so-called colonial reforms of those years did not include all Angolans and in some cases the reforms were accompanied by land dispossession under the myth of bringing agricultural development to rural areas. During this time of reform, some people were dispossessed of their land to make room for white settlers (Bender 2004).

In sum, the Portuguese colonial reformers were not motivated by a genuine desire to fully integrate black Angolans into the country's economic, cultural and political life but the reforms came about as a defence mechanism against growing international pressure on Portugal to free the colonies. Ironically, the period of reform was characterised by excessive political repressions by the notorious Portuguese secret police, the PIDE (International and State Defence Police). The PIDE inflicted a culture of fear and distrust among Angolans, with its arbitrary imprisonments and torture of any Angolan suspected of harbouring anti-colonial sentiments (Henderson 1979). Such tactics contradicted the Portuguese myth of a benevolent colonial system which protected the human rights of all Angolans, irrespective of race (Almeida and Corkill 2015).

4.6 Myths of the non-racist Portuguese colonial system

Lusotropicalism has it that, in the Portuguese colonies, whites, blacks and mixed-race persons lived in harmony without any racial prejudice. This supposed harmony was based on four distinctive myths.

The first myth was that of the non-racist society.[29] Racism was something that other colonial powers in Africa practiced. The Portuguese colonial system accepted the so-called native as part of Portugal. Thus, whatever problems the colonies had were interpreted as economically related and easily solvable if Portuguese colonialism continued with economic development reforms (Castelo 1998). By dismissing race and substituting it with economic problems, the Portuguese colonial regime wanted to generalise that any economic problem was a problem that affected all who lived in the colonies, irrespective of race (Bender 2004). According to Portuguese colonial logic, the fact that poor whites could also be found in Portugal was an indication that the colonial system was non-racist. The struggle was for economic equality rather than race discrimination because the Portuguese by 'nature' were non-racial (Bender 2004). As the argument goes, if race were a problem in the Portuguese colonies, interracial relationships would not have happened with the frequency that they did (Castelo 1998). According to the colonial regime and the myth of Lusotropicalism, the existence of interracial families was proof that the Portuguese colonial system was non-racial. However, Bender (2004) states that interracial relationships were not exceptional to the Portuguese colonial system; British colonies like Jamaica had experienced interracial relationships at a higher rate than Angola. The only place where interracial relationships were somewhat higher was Cape Verde (Bender 2004), but here Cohen and Toninato (2010) pointed out that most of the Portuguese who ended up in Cape

---

29 The myth of the non-racial colonial system continues to dominate Portuguese society even today, despite evidence of racism in certain sectors of Portuguese society (Almeida and Corkill 2015).

Verde were of Jewish descent and had been expelled from Portugal. Moreover, the mode of the colonial system implemented in Cape Verde was less oppressive than that of other colonies, so much so that Cape Verdeans did not resort to an armed struggle for independence. Within the hierarchised Portuguese colonial system, Cape Verdeans were often treated better than those in the other colonies (Bender 2004).

One plausible explanation for mixed-race populations in the Portuguese colonies could be the gender imbalance (Bender 2004). In other words, there were more Portuguese white men going to the colonies than women, even if the ratio changed slightly in Angola in the 1950s when the migration of Portuguese white women became more frequent (Bender 2004). Similar dynamics are also observable in other colonial systems, where mixed-race relations were common because of a surfeit of males (Warwick 2003). Thus, the notion that mixed race was indicative of a non-racial Portuguese colonial system and that it was unique to Portuguese colonialism, like Lusotropicalism, was a myth. It is safe to argue that the 'production' of mixed-race people in the Portuguese and other colonies came as a result of biological need rather than being indicative of a non-racial colonial system.

The second myth was the Portuguese capacity to culturally assimilate in the colonies. De Sousa Santos (2002) states that the Portuguese had the capacity to adapt in the colonies better than other European colonial powers due to the fact that Portugal was part of the 'semi-periphery' within the world system and hence less industrialised than other colonial powers. Moreover, within Europe, Portuguese citizens were also discriminated against and considered as second-class citizens because they were not felt to be 'white enough' (de Sousa Santos 2002). According to de Sousa Santos, other Europeans from Northern countries visiting Portugal were often amazed at the dark complexion of Portuguese citizens and the underdevelopment in Portugal. He further argues that Portugal was not really a colonial power like Britain or France because of its less-developed economy but, rather, it was somehow posing as a colonial power. In other words, Portugal did not have the economic means to be a proper colonial power. Although de Sousa Santos' (2002) argument makes sense regarding Portugal's peripheral position within Europe, its weaker economic strength and its inability to fully control its colonies, nevertheless his arguments are questionable, in particular when it comes to the notion of Portuguese cultural assimilation in the colonies.[30] Historical evidence from Protestant missionaries working in rural areas in Angola during the Portuguese colonial period indicates that the Portuguese colonial system was ignorant of the local customs in Angola (Henderson 1979). Portuguese colonialists had little interest in learning anything from black Africans because they considered them to be backward and inferior (Bender 2004); the expectation was that those considered primitive would assimilate into the Portuguese superior culture. The Portuguese colonial stance of *Estado Novo* strongly encouraged black Africans to abandon their supposed primitive culture and languages and adopt the Portuguese 'way of life' (Bender 2004; Jerónimo 2015). This included speaking Portuguese well, dressing and eating food in the manner of the Portuguese. The majority were expected to adapt to the minority culture (Duffy 1962). At the heart of the assimilation of the 'native' was the ideology that the culturally despised black Angolans were not considered to have anything of importance to contribute to Portuguese colonialists apart from forced labour (Bender 2004; Jerónimo 2015). In fact, the Portuguese colonial system demanded that black Angolans who wanted to be considered as citizens had to go through a process of assimilation – a bureaucratic ritual which required them, among other things, to have a Portuguese name, speak Portuguese fluently and have the ability to pay taxes (Bender 2004).

Even though black Angolans obtained the status of assimilates, in practice they were not fully accepted; instead, they were pejoratively called *calcinhas*[31] (Nascimento 2016). Moreover, the Portuguese colonial system did not create the conditions to assimilate all Angolans. The system itself was selective and only rewarded a chosen few, mostly from urban places; those who did not make it had to resort to a Protestant education (Bender 2004). Protestant missionaries coming from predominantly English-speaking countries faced significant opposition from the Portuguese colonial regime in Angola because they were accused of having a 'subversive' education sys-

---

30 The topic of Portuguese adaptability in the colonies was mentioned by some of my Portuguese migrant participants in Lubango. They said that coming to Angola was not a problem because, historically, the Portuguese tended to go abroad and adapt in any given context.

31 *Calcinhas*, literally translated, means little trousers but, during Portuguese colonialism, it was used as a pejorative term to refer to black Angolans who had gone through a process of civilisation and had later adopted the Portuguese colonial way of life (Nascimento 2016). The idea behind the term was to say that black Angolans who had obtained their status of *assimilados* by having a Portuguese identity card could never be real Portuguese.

tem[32] which impeded black Africans from fully assimilating into Portuguese culture (Soremekun 1965). The myth of the Portuguese capacity to adopt and adapt the culture of the colonised did not take into account the fact that interactions between Portuguese colonialists and the colonised were dominated by power relations of master and servant. The latter was expected to assimilate into the master's way of life, to act and behave by imitating the master. Therefore, de Sousa Santos' (2002) argument is questionable in the light of these historical facts.

The third myth is that of the benevolent Portuguese colonial system. This system strongly believed that its colonial methods were beneficial to black Africans. The benevolent nature of Portuguese colonialism dismissed any atrocities committed in its name and emphasised instead the 'positive' elements of colonialism (Castelo 1998). Yet Protestant missionaries (British, Swiss and North American) working in rural areas of Angola during Portuguese colonialism characterised the system as brutal and inhuman (Soremekun 1965). The brutality was evident in the aggressive nature of the recruitment of cheap black labour to sustain the coffee industry and the use of indentured labour on the sugar plantations on the islands of São Tomé and Príncipe (Henderson 1979; Soremekun 1965). Even after the abolition of transatlantic slavery in 1807, Portuguese colonies continued illegally transporting human cargo until 1850 and only stopped after British cruise ships began patrolling the Portuguese colonial coasts (Luce 1990). However, internally, other forms of slavery continued to be practiced, the most commonly known being forced labour, which was just as brutal as the slavery (Byam 1997). In defence of these oppressive and inhuman practices, Portuguese colonial apologists argued that forced labour was necessary for the economic development of the colony as well as for the human development of black Angolans, in particular the inculcation of the work ethic, which was assumed to be one of the traits that black Angolans did not possess (Henderson 1979). The Portuguese colonial regime undoubtedly used oppressive methods and justified them as part of its civilising mission

---

32 This subversive education system included teaching in local languages and, sometimes, in English. The Portuguese colonial regime saw this as an affront to their control over the colony as well as impeding the assimilation project which required the negation of usage of an African language (Soremekun 1965). Furthermore, the fact that these missions strategically located themselves in areas that were ravaged by recruitment for slavery and later for forced labour was also viewed with great suspicion by the Portuguese colonial regime (Birmingham 2006). In other words, the colonial regime saw the presence of Protestant missionaries as a multiple threat.

(Jerónimo 2015). At the heart of the Portuguese colonial ideology was the notion that it was the Portuguese colonial duty to bring the 'childlike' black Africans to a higher development stage, even if that included the violation of basic human rights. In other words, 'the end justified the means'; however, in reality, the Portuguese colonial system was far from benevolent (Birmingham 2006).

The fourth myth was that Portuguese colonialism brought education and civilisation to native Angolans. However, in the case of Angola, Bender (2004) points out that, in the 1950s, 97 per cent of the enrolment in the 37 high schools was white and that all black Angolans of 15 years and older were illiterate. Black Angolans who managed to obtain an education did so in the much-reviled Protestant missionary schools.[33] Bender (2004) compares the Portuguese colonial education system with that of the British African colonies and concludes that even countries like South Africa and Zimbabwe (the former Rhodesia), with their racial segregation polices, had more black African students enrolled than Angola under Portuguese colonialism. The plausible explanation for this imbalance could be found in the stratification of the Portuguese colonial labour market. According to Henderson (1990), the Portuguese colonial education system was not designed to cater for all Angolans but mainly for whites. The few black Angolans who managed to break through the educational barriers were either exceptional or had strong support from Protestant missions. This was one of the reasons why the Protestant missions were in constant conflict with the Portuguese colonial regime. Protestant mission schools were accused of diverting black Angolans away from doing 'proper' work by encouraging education, which was seen as a waste of time (Soremekun 1965). It is not surprising that most of the postcolonial educated elite came from mission schools. Similar educational dynamics were evident in the Portuguese colony of Mozambique (Macamo 2005). Therefore, the notion that the Portuguese colonial system promoted the education and civilisation of

---

33 Protestant missionary schools played crucial roles in the education of black Angolans. While the Portuguese system of education limited black Angolans to only studying up to the fourth grade, Protestant mission education encouraged them to study beyond the limitation of Portuguese colonialism. As such, some of the first black Angolan university graduates came from Protestant missions. The Portuguese colonial system basically reduced the education of black Angolans to the ability to read and write. Moreover, Protestant mission schools were also considered subversive because they used vernacular language as part of the education, which Portuguese colonialists considered to hinder the process of assimilation of black Angolans (Soremekun 1965).

black Angolans was a total myth – in fact, its economic system reduced black Angolans to manual labour; there was the belief that black Angolans were better suited to certain tasks that did not include thinking, administration, management and leadership – those positions were reserved for whites (Henderson 1979; Jerónimo 2015). The Portuguese colonial system was concerned with using black bodies as a human cargo for slavery and forced labour. Despite the realities presented above, Lusotropicalism and Portuguese colonialism have still not been dealt with properly in Portugal. Lusotropicalism as a discourse and ideology continues to indirectly dominate the country, especially when it comes to issues of black immigrants and the relations of Portugal with its former colonies in Africa.

4.7 Lusotropicalism in postcolonial Portugal and black migration

Lusotropicalism, as demonstrated above, was a myth that was not based on the reality of how the Portuguese colonial system functioned. Despite its dismissal as a myth, some tenets of Lusotropicalism did not disappear in Portugal after the end of colonialism but continued to be part of national behaviour, attitudes and identity (Almeida and Corkill 2015). There are two Lusotropicalist principles that continue to be held in some sectors of Portuguese society. These are, firstly, racism being seen as a problem of other European countries and, secondly, colonialism as a forgotten topic in Portuguese memory. Let us consider each of these in turn.

According to Fikes (2009), racism continues to be a taboo topic in Portuguese society and is viewed mainly as a problem of other European countries. Such an understanding of racism draws directly from the legacy of Lusotropicalism in Portugal (Vala, Lopes and Lima 2008). Portugal continues to project an image of a non-racial country and depicts itself as one with a long history of multiculturalism (Castelo 1998). Arguably, there is some legitimacy for the Portuguese to believe that racism is not (or is less of) a problem in Portuguese society, based on analyses of the European Social Survey and other datasets. Vala *et al.* (2008) demonstrated that the heritage of Lusotropicalism appears to enable the Portuguese population to express a lower level of racism than all the other 14 countries of the pre-2004 European Community. Instead, the expression of 'cultural inferiority' towards the 'other' is voiced in a more covert way. In other words, racism in Portugal could be described as what Bonilla-Silva (2006: 29) called 'racism without racism and without racists', which is a form of colour-blind racism based on particular cultural stereotypes of a group and serves as a justification for why some groups lag behind economically. Most of my Portuguese participants would describe Portugal as a welcoming country without racism, where people from different backgrounds live in peace together – they attribute such an attitude to the supposed positive nature of Portuguese colonialism.

Secondly, if race is a taboo topic in Portugal, as suggested by Fikes (2009), so Portuguese colonialism is also a forgotten memory. According to Castelo (1998), Portuguese colonial history tends not to fixate too much on Portuguese historical memory. When it does, it does not focus too much on the plight of black Africans under Portuguese colonialism. There is, in a sense, a gap in how Portuguese colonial history is understood in the Portuguese collective memory (Castelo 1998). There is not much emphasis on the role of the Portuguese in the slave trade, forced labour, the caste-like colonial educational system and other social hierarchies (Bender 2004). Instead, Portuguese colonial memory tends to concentrate on the positive aspects of the Portuguese voyages of discovery, the civilising mission and the cultural legacy of Portugal in the former colonies (Castelo 1998). As such, Portuguese colonialism is still romanticised and positively presented as a great achievement by a small country. The idea is that Portugal is endowed with few economic resources but with a great sense of duty to spread Western civilisation and Christianity to the rest of the world (Birmingham 2006). It was not surprising to hear this perspective from Jose in Lisbon, defending Portuguese colonialism based on his childhood memory of living in Angola. Jose was a *retornado*, a returned white settler from Angola. He said:

> *Portuguese colonialism was not bad; the Portuguese built roads and schools and civilised the black Angolans. Racism was never part of Portuguese colonialism. I remember playing with black Angolan friends and I went to the same school, where there was no racism. But then, the communists started planting these ideas of independence and racism in the minds of the black Angolans. That is when all the racism noise started. After independence, the economy collapsed and all the blacks wanted to come to Portugal and seek asylum. Portugal opened the doors for them but some of them keep on complaining about racism. Portugal was never a racist country; we are open to everyone – look at Lisbon. Here in Lisbon we have African migrants from everywhere and we all live together in a peaceful way. And now we have Portuguese companies going to Angola in order to rebuild it* (Jose, Lisbon, July 2016).

For Jose, the Portuguese colonial memory was reduced to socialisation between blacks and whites and there is not much reflection on the subservient positions of blacks and the conditions of structural racism that existed under Portuguese colonialism. For him, the focus is mostly on socialisation and semi-integrated schools. In other words, for Jose the fact that the wall that separated people based on colour lines was not visible is proof that Portuguese colonialism was not racist.

Jose's experience of Portuguese colonialism is related to what Almeida and Corkill (2015) have demonstrated concerning Portuguese society's understanding of its colonialism. These authors argue that Portuguese society has taken a less-critical view of Portuguese colonialism because black Africans were not as visible in Portuguese society after the end of colonialism. They further opine that Portuguese society was somewhat homogenous and those who came to Portugal after the fall of colonialism were predominantly white. One can extend this argument further by pointing out how the dramatic scenes of independence and the chaotic way that the majority of white settlers left the colonies have shaped the discourse of Portuguese colonialism. This kind of discourse tends to focus on the plight of the *retornados* who left the colonies rather than focusing on the colonial violence which black Africans endured under Portuguese colonialism. Attesting to this, Jose says: '*My father left everything in Angola and came back here with only a suitcase; the* Calcinhas *took everything*'. Thus, there are nostalgic memories in certain circles of Portuguese society, as well as in Angola, that Portuguese colonialism was not so bad in comparison to the postcolonial civil war (Åkesson 2018).

The civil war and subsequent economic deterioration during the 1980s and early 1990s and the migrations from former African colonies to Portugal had somehow hindered the possibility for the country to look critically at its historical memory of its colonial system. Instead, the focus shifted to the plight of black Africans seeking refuge in Portugal in the postcolonial context. For many former white settlers who returned to Portugal, like Jose, the influx of black migrants was more like a self-fulfilling prophecy that was predicted by those who did not want to see Angolan independence. According to Birmingham (2006), one argument used to keep the Portuguese colonies was that black Africans were not yet ready for self-government and the Portuguese presence in Africa was a factor that maintained peace and stability among the different ethnic groups, in addition to bringing economic development. The influx of African migrants from the former colonies is then used to justify the 'Afro-pessimism' that dominated some sectors of Portuguese society. According to Almeida and

Corkill (2015), the skin colour of the migrants and their visibility challenged the old myth that Portugal was not a racist country; however, it also re-opened some old colonial social hierarchies. Pereira (2010) relates how black migrants occupied the lowest strata of Portuguese society when it came to employment. Most of the challenges which black migrants faced stemmed from sectors such as housing, employment and education (Fikes 2009). However, racism in Portugal, on the structural level, is always interpreted as economic deprivation rather than as an innate social problem. In other words, just like the colonial period, the Portuguese state continues to interpret racism primarily as an economic rather than a structural social problem and thus as an issue that can easily be solved with better housing, better employment and better education for black migrants. It is not far-fetched to argue that this interpretation by the authorities of racism as an economic problem is rooted in the historical myth of Lusotropicalism and its essentialised discourse, which understands race as not part of Portuguese colonialism and society (Almeida and Corkill 2015). Thus, the survival of Lusotropicalism in modern Portugal works to project a positive image of the Portuguese colonial system in these postcolonial times. As such, when interacting with Portuguese interlocutors in Lisbon, the focus tends to be on the mythical relationship that Portugal had with its former colonies. Based on a common language that is Portuguese, Lusotropicalism is presented as a factor that unites Portugal and its former colonies (Cahen 2012).

4.8 Postcolonial Lusotropicalism and the linguistic legacy in Angola

Although Portuguese colonialism officially ended long ago, the indirect presence of Portugal in Angola continues through various legacies. It was not just the former conservative Prime Minister Passos Coelho who encouraged Portuguese citizens to 'grasp the opportunities of the Portuguese language market and migrate to former colonies', as Pereira and Azevedo (2019: 11) have suggested. Most of my Portuguese migrant informants in Lubango link their migration trajectory to the factor of the Portuguese language:

> *My decision to come to Angola was also influenced by the Portuguese language. I could have gone to other countries but it would have taken me another year to learn the language before finding a job; but coming to Angola there was no need to learn another language – everyone here seems to speak and understand Portuguese; even people on the street speak funny but one*

can understand what they are trying to say (Ana-Maria, Lubango, September 2015).

In this context, the Portuguese language functions as a form of social capital that helps to quickly integrate Portuguese migrants into the Angolan job market.

Schubert (2017) links the influence of the Portuguese language in contemporary Angola to the modernist socialist ideology adopted by the postcolonial government of the MPLA, which discouraged the use of African languages and considered them a sign of obscurantism and tribalism. Schubert's analysis could be just one of the possibilities, however; the usage of the Portuguese language could also be linked to the Portuguese colonial legacy of forced assimilation which rejected African languages and associated them with a lack of culture and intelligence (Bender 2004). As mentioned before, most postcolonial elites went through the process of assimilation to the extent that, after the end of the colonial war, the Portuguese colonial army was surprised that members of the MPLA had so much in common with them in terms of language, culture and etiquette (Cahen 2012). Moreover, the strong Afro-pessimism which characterises much of the Portuguese colonial system might have played a significant role in the postcolonial Angolan government's language policies. It is not mere speculation to suggest that postcolonial Angolan elites had a similar distaste for African languages as the colonial regime, given the modernist socialist ideology which was concerned to unite the postcolonial nation under one common language.

One of the problems which will be discussed later in the thesis was the association of the Portuguese language with, culturally speaking, being a 'real' Angolan (Shubert 2017). In other words, the new political elite composed of white Angolans, mixed-race persons and black assimilates continues to indirectly implement colonial polices of associating those who speak Portuguese with the 'real citizens' of Angola, thus replicating the same old social hierarchies inherited from colonial times. The option to officially use Portuguese and dismiss the use of African languages was taken in order to present a united country with a myth of common descent. The question here is not so much the adoption of Portuguese as the official language of postcolonial Angola but, rather, the implied notion that those who did not speak Portuguese could not be considered Angolans. Such a myth is somehow connected to the oppressive stance of assimilation during Portuguese colonialism (Moco 2015). It is not surprising that many postcolonial Angolans see their exceptionalism to the rest of Africa as based on having Portuguese as a mother tongue and their inability to communicate in other

African languages (Moco 2015; Soares de Oliveira 2015). As such, the Portuguese language in postcolonial Angola functions as a marker that separates the different social classes, educational levels and layers of cultural sophistication (Shubert 2017). In some cases, the Portuguese language is the way that postcolonial elites demonstrate their sense of cultural sophistication and closeness to Portugal (Cahen 2012). The Portuguese language in Angola also serves as a way to draw boundaries between 'civilised' and 'uncivilised' and between 'citizens' and 'non-citizens', just as it did under the Portuguese colonial system. Being Angolan continues to be associated with the ability to speak Portuguese.[34]

Portuguese is indeed one of the most spoken languages in postcolonial Angola but there are other African languages that are used in rural areas and in places where the Portuguese colonial influence was not as deep as it was in places like Luanda and other coastal towns (Cahen 2012). These African languages tend to play a secondary role in Angola. For many migrants – like Ana-Maria, quoted above – going to Angola is like going to a place that seems familiar as they are even able to understand Angolans who do not speak Portuguese fluently. In the colonial imaginary, the ability of Ana-Maria to communicate in Portuguese with people on the streets makes it appear that the Portuguese colonial assimilation policies have indeed worked and that there is a certain proximity between Portugal and Angola based on a shared language. However, the evidence below shows a different story. The Portuguese language legacy is not necessarily the result of an effective Portuguese colonial system but is also a result of other factors like internal migration from rural to urban areas.

4.8.1 The other side of the Portuguese language legacy in postcolonial Angola

The fact that the Portuguese language continues to dominate postcolonial Angola might suggest that Portuguese colonial assimilation policies were

---

34 During fieldwork, I met an Angolan from the province of Moxico who was born in the province that borders Zambia. He left Angola for Zambia in the 1970s as a refugee and thus grew up and did his primary studies there. After the end of the Angolan conflict, he wanted to apply for Angolan citizenship but could not get it because he could not speak Portuguese. He shared with me that the officials told him that he cannot be Angolan if he does not speak Portuguese. Ironically, he spoke the local language but that was not good enough to convince the authorities.

successful because, nowadays, Portuguese is widely spoken. However, as Bender (2004) pointed out, Portuguese colonial language policy was a failure because it only included a select number of blacks. Nevertheless, what the Portuguese colonial system failed to achieve the postcolonial government managed to indirectly achieve. Moco (2015) argues that the Portuguese language is more widely spoken today in Angola than it was under Portuguese colonialism. One of the reasons is migration from rural to urban areas as a consequence of the postcolonial civil war, which had a direct impact on encouraging the relocation of internally displaced people and Luanda was one place that could offer security. Luanda can be considered as the bastion of Portuguese colonial legacy and a place where the Portuguese language tends to dominate. According to Schubert (2017), foreigners who do not speak Portuguese in urban areas like Luanda tend to be treated as outsiders and pejoratively called *Langa*[35] or *Mamadou*.[36] The same treatment is applied to Angolans from rural areas who speak Portuguese with a particular accent. They are called names like *Bailundo* and *Sulano*.[37] The inability to communicate properly in Portuguese, especially in urban places like Luanda, is associated with all kinds of colonial stereotypes and stigma such as being uneducated, uncivilised and an outsider. Thus, there is social pressure to speak Portuguese to a good standard in order to be accepted in certain circles (Moco 2015). Many of these dynamics are traceable through the strong Portuguese colonial divide between urban and rural areas (Bender 2004). As suggested by Nascimento (2016), during Portuguese colonial times, urban spaces were reserved for white settlers and the blacks were located on the outskirts or *musseques*.[38] However, blacks in *musseques* were taught to believe that they are better than those in rural areas because they could express themselves in Portuguese and behave in a more civilised manner. Some of these dynamics continued to

---

35 The word *Langa* is pejoratively used to describe migrants from the Democratic Republic of Congo (DRC) or the Republic of Congo Brazzaville. *Langa* at times can also include Angolans who live in areas that border with the DRC, given the linguistic and cultural proximity of Angolans who migrated there then returned to Angola.

36 The word *Mamadou* is pejoratively used to describe migrants from West Africa, in particular from French-speaking areas, who have different tuck shops in Luanda and other provinces. *Mamadou* can also mean a Muslim from West Africa.

37 The words *Bailundo* and *Sulano* are pejoratively used to describe people from the South, in particular from the highland provinces of Huambo and Bie. These words are also used to describe members of UNITA.

38 *Musseques* are the slums located around the city of Luanda.

play a role in postcolonial Angola (Moco 2015). The status of the Portuguese language there is, in some cases, associated with a colonial understating of belonging (Moco 2015). Under Portuguese colonialism, those who spoke Portuguese well and fulfilled other requirements were considered citizens of the empire whilst, under the postcolonial state, they were and are considered real Angolans (Bender 2004; Moco 2015).

The adoption of the Portuguese language in postcolonial Angola was meant to unite the country under socialist modernist ideology but it had a different effect, which was a perpetuation of old colonial social and geographical hierarchies. The geographical divides were those based on differences between the littoral and the hinterland and between urban and rural areas, already evident under Portuguese colonialism (Schubert 2017). In postcolonial Angola, those living in urban areas continued to feel superior to those in rural areas. Social hierarchies were built on differences between civilised and uncivilised, between black and white and between blacks and those of mixed race. The geographical hierarchies were largely dominated by economic differences whilst the social hierarchies were dependent on the ability of a person to communicate properly in Portuguese and be conversant with Portuguese culture and etiquette (Moco 2015). These dynamics intersect with each other and, in some cases, depend on context. However, it is clear that they continue to dominate postcolonial Angolan society as a means to exclude and include. In spite of the existence of these hierarchies, the postcolonial Angolan government continues to believe in and insist on the myth that the Portuguese language is a factor that unites Angolans of different social and economic strata without acknowledging the colonial legacy linked to the Portuguese language. It is not surprising, then, that the Portuguese government uses the Portuguese language as a factor that unites the former colonisers and the colonised (Cahen 2012). The next sub-section shows how the myth of the Portuguese language as a factor uniting not only the Angolans among themselves but also Portugal and the rest of the former colonies was institutionalised by Portugal without addressing the historical and oppressive nature of the Portuguese language.

4.8.2 The institutionalisation of the Portuguese language in the former colonies

The loss of the colonies left a significant vacuum in Portugal's status in the global arena as well as Portuguese national consciousness. As mentioned before, the country did not want to relinquish its overseas provinces. Although the connections between Portugal and its former colonies continued through various networks, there was a need to restore a symbolic Portuguese colonial influence and presence in the former colonies. One of the ways that the Portuguese state found to continue to maintain such a presence was through the foundation of the CPLP (*Comunidades dos Paises de Lingua Portuguesa* or Community of Portuguese-Speaking Countries), set up by the Portuguese government on 17 July 1996 with the goal to unite the former colonies through the Portuguese language. It functions somewhat like a 'commonwealth' of Portuguese-speaking countries (Castelo 1998). Cahen (2012) states that some of the founders of the CPLP have argued that the organisation had effectively already existed since Portuguese colonialism and that 1996 was only the official institutionalisation of it. In other words, the Portuguese government always forged fraternal bonds with its colonies based on a common language. However, scholars like Castelo (1998) critically argue that the CPLP's foundation is based on Lusotropicalism – in particular, on the idea of seeing the Portuguese language as a vinculum that unites former colonies. Furthermore, Cahen (2012) links the foundation of the CPLP to Lusotropicalism in that the CPLP is there to primarily defend the linguistic interests of Portugal – especially the preservation of the Portuguese language in the former colonies in the 'Tropics'. There is a sort of latent imperialistic motive behind the founding of the CPLP, as well as a subtle commitment to promote the Portuguese economic and cultural legacy in former colonies, best facilitated through the active use of the Portuguese language.

However, one problem with the CPLP lies in the lack of reflexivity on the role of the Portuguese language in creating social hierarchies during Portuguese colonialism and in postcolonial times. There is a dehistoricisation of the Portuguese language whereby it is presented as a fundamentalist notion articulating the language as something that has magically fallen from heaven to unite the different colonies. There is not enough engagement with the past and how the Portuguese language was used under the colonial system as a means to exclude and deny citizenship to blacks who were considered to be uncivilised unless they spoke Portuguese. There is no recognition of the value of African languages, nor of the possibility that the Portuguese connection with its former colonies can transcend the single common denominator of language. This gives the impression that the Portuguese language is above all other languages in the former colonies. One can argue that the CPLP is the reincarnation of a kind of 'soft' Lusotropicalism because, among other things, it uses the discourse of common descent, common culture, harmony and unity (Cahen 2012). It is not surprising that some Portuguese migrants in Lubango kept on highlighting the fact that *Portugal e Angola são povos irmãos* (Portugal and Angola are fraternal brothers), which echoes the Lusotropicalist sentiment of shared fraternity through a common language. These and other factors contribute to the notion that the Portuguese language legacy should continue because it brings the former colonies together in spite of an existing cultural diversity that the CPLP tends to overlook. Therefore, it is fair to say that the CPLP is more connected with black assimilates or the elites than to common citizens and does not do justice to the linguistic realities and complexities of the former colonies. However, this is not the only legacy that still affects these former colonies. In the case of Angola, the Portuguese colonial legacy also plays a significant role in what I call a politics of names.

4.8.3 The politics of Portuguese names in postcolonial Angola

Another important linguistic legacy that is linked to Portuguese colonialism is the politics of names in postcolonial Angola. Unlike other countries in Africa where 'African' names are well regarded and, in some cases, symbolise belonging to a particular geographical area and/or ethnic group, as suggested by Lentz (2013), the postcolonial politics of names in Angola tends to be slightly different in that it is connected to Portuguese colonialism. Under the myth of creating a state devoid of tribalism in Angola, African names are often shunned and are considered to be a sign of obscurantism.[39] Instead, Portuguese names in postcolonial Angola were believed to symbolise modernity, progress and civilisation (Moco 2015). There is an unwritten rule in Angola that to be a true Angolan is to have Portuguese-sounding names, while to have an African name is a sign of backwardness.

---

39 According to Schubert (2017), certain Portuguese names in Angola are connected with Angolan black and mixed-race elites who have a long history of interaction and commerce with Portuguese settlers. Some of these elites started losing power after the arrival of new Portuguese colonial settlers. Relegated to second-class citizens, they fought back by joining the anti-colonial struggle against the Portuguese regime. After independence, some of the elites were able to regain political and economic power. It should also be mentioned that, during the anti-colonial struggles, some MPLA officials took up African nicknames of war (Mabeko-Tali 2018).

One Angolan informant, Alfredo, who studied in Namibia and South Africa, complained about how the politics of names works in Angola:

There is a political attempt here in Angola to make us all creolos. I am serious, this is not some kind of conspiracy theory. Look, I lived in Namibia and South Africa and blacks used their African names and they speak their languages without feeling shame. But here in the cities it is different. Portuguese names are considered Angolan and Angolan names are rejected. I can give you an example: when the baby of my sister was born she wanted to give the baby an African name but the registrar would not allow it. He said the name was too African and was not on the official list of acceptable names for babies. You see, they have a list of acceptable names at the notary office and the official told my sister that, if the baby was to take up the African name, the baby will suffer bullying at school because the name is too difficult to pronounce. But if she chooses a different name, like Pedro or Fernando, it would not be a problem to register the baby at all. I found it interesting that the name suggested by my sister was rejected for being too African but names like Pedro and Fernando are considered Angolan names. Can you imagine this? Colonialism is over but we still apply colonial laws, we are still thinking that only Portuguese names are beautiful. Sorry but we cannot continue to be like that. Blacks in Namibia and South African have African names and they are proud of that but here it is not acceptable (Alfredo, Lubango, September 2015).

Alfredo's frustration with the politics of names in postcolonial Angola comes from his experience of living in other African countries, where having African names or speaking an African language were not considered signs of obscurantism. Moreover, he also connects the politics of names to a continuation of old colonial laws and the notion that only Portuguese names can be considered Angolan. Mamdani (1996) argues that postcolonial states are, in many ways, a reflection of colonial states and certain colonial practices were transferred to postcolonial states by the political and economic elites without proper contextualisation. In the case of the politics of names in Angola, there is a direct link to old colonial assimilation policies which demanded that black Angolans change their African names into Portuguese ones as part of the 'civilisation' process. Alfredo, who is also a member of the opposition party in Lubango, was probably aware of the connections of the politics of names with Portuguese colonial policies.

In some cases, Angolans from rural areas feel compelled to change their African names into Portuguese-sounding names in order to be accepted

(Moco 2015). It is not surprising that most postcolonial Angolans say they come from Luanda when they are asked where they come from and tend to take pride in their Portuguese names. This is done in order to avoid the stigma of being associated with coming from a rural area, commonly called *da provincia*.[40] Besides this, there is also a political reason why some Angolans prefer to have Portuguese names and change their place of origin. Having a Portuguese name is one way to avoid being associated with opposition parties. This is the case particularly with names from the highlands of Angola that were historically associated with UNITA (Moco 2015). Interestingly, while doing research in Lubango and Lisbon, it was not uncommon for Portuguese participants and even local Angolans to question my (first) name because, according to them, it did not sound Angolan. '*Are you really Angolan? Because your name does not sound like Angolan, it sounds like* Mamadou'. Some Angolan participants only calmed down when I mentioned my surname and they heard me speaking Portuguese.

The question is not so much about whether African names are rejected in postcolonial Angola, because certain African names from certain regions like Luanda tend to be accepted, depending on who is using them. It is more a question of class, as those associated with the elite can also have African names without being questioned. According to Mabeko-Tali (2018), there was a time during the war against Portuguese colonialism that members of the MPLA intentionally adopted African names. Nevertheless, after independence and the struggle to build a new nation, things changed. In the context of the civil conflict, the MPLA distanced itself from all things 'African', which were associated with the opposition UNITA and FNLA. Moco (2015) points out that, during the Angolan conflict, African names were stereotypically used to identify who the enemy was or who was suspected of not being Angolan enough according to the constructed socialist modernist idea of Angolan that the MPLA government wanted to portray. Thus, one can argue that the politics of names in postcolonial Angola is associated with three elements: firstly, the colonial legacy of civilisation; secondly, the Angolan conflict and its geographical div-

---

40 Many Angolans prefer to associate themselves with urban places like Luanda rather than rural places. There is a stigma associated with being from outside of the capital. Being from Luanda gives a sense of prestige and superiority. It is more like saying that only those born in the capital are true Angolans. There is a saying in Angola that goes '*Angola e' Luanda, Lobito e jardim; do resto e campim*' which can be translated as: 'Angola is Luanda and Lobito is a garden; the rest is grass'.

ision; and, thirdly, the divide between urban and rural areas, which can be traceable to Portuguese colonial geographical hierarchies.

These hierarchies continue to play a significant role in Angola. Places on or close to the coast, with historically stronger Portuguese colonial influence, tend to be considered as more civilised, with better development, while the rural areas of the interior of the country have always been neglected (Moco 2015). According to Bender (2004), the Portuguese colonial system used the divide between urban and rural regions to tell black Angolans in urban centres that they were better than those in the villages, who were seen as *atrasados* (backward). This colonial legacy continues to manifest itself in postcolonial Angola, where having a Portuguese name is still indirectly associated with being 'urban'. The next section looks at how the Portuguese legacy also extends into other areas such as family networks.

4.9 The legacy of family networks in postcolonial Angola

The Portuguese colonial legacy in Angola is also dominated by a history of family networks. As mentioned before, some studies conducted on Angola tend to downplay the role of family networks, in particular those of white and mixed-race Angolans. However, in order to understand Portuguese migration to Angola, it is important to include reference to family networks because some of the recent Portuguese migration to Angola is linked to this. In the case of Lubango, there are white Angolans, many of them managers in private-sector businesses, who have helped to find employment for struggling relatives in Portugal.

> *We moved back to Lubango because my husband's father has a company here. When my husband lost his job we decided to move here; we do not intend to move back to Portugal because the children are happy and there is also a Portuguese school here* (Sofia, Lubango, September 2015).

The existence and legacy of family networks might be viewed by Lusotropicalism enthusiasts as an indication that Portugal's colonial system was indeed exceptional. However, Angolan family networks with Portugal are quite complex because the phenomenon is divided into different categories.

The first category is white Angolans with a long historical presence in Angola, in some cases three to four generations. Some of these white Angolans do not have any connections to Portugal at all apart from skin colour.[41] The second group is composed of white Angolans who married Portuguese migrants and moved to Angola after the end of the war in 2002 and after the global economic crisis of 2008; there are also white Portuguese married to black or mixed-race Angolans.[42] The third group are mixed-race families who still have contact with their Portuguese relatives and who enjoy the benefits of having a Portuguese passport and transnational privileges. However, it is important to mention that not every mixed-race Angolan family is connected to families in Portugal. The fourth group are white Angolans – born in Angola but raised in Portugal – who have returned to Angola as Portuguese migrants and are eligible in some cases to apply for Angolan citizenship.[43] The fifth group are black Angolan-Portuguese, born and raised in Portugal to Angolan parents. Sixth are black Angolans born in Angola who migrated to Portugal as asylum-seekers and who have obtained Portuguese citizenship and returned to Angola. All these groups are directly and indirectly linked to Portuguese migration to Angola.

There are two important characteristics of some of these groups. The first is their transnational propensity. Some white, mixed-race and black Angolans with Portuguese passports have had the privilege to live in both Portugal and Angola depending on the economic and political situation of the two countries, as already noted earlier. During times of economic difficulty in Portugal they moved to Angola; when the economic situation looked difficult in Angola, they moved back to Portugal. The second characteristic is the switch of identities. White Angolans sometimes present themselves as Portuguese when the situation is convenient.

I moved here to Angola because my husband comes from here. When the economic situation deteriorated in Portugal we decided to move back to Angola. But this is not our first time in Angola. Some years ago we were in Luanda

---

41 While looking for participants in Lubango, I came across several white Angolans who were very disappointed when I asked if they were Portuguese. One particular individual told me that he has never been to Portugal and never been outside of Africa.

42 Most of the marriages among the participants were between white Angolans and white Portuguese migrants. There was one between a white Portuguese migrant and an Angolan of mixed race and one between a Portuguese migrant and a black Angolan.

43 Some members of these groups see themselves as Angolans while others see themselves as Portuguese. Åkesson (2018) seems to associate all of them with being Portuguese, regardless of their claims to be Angolans.

but this time we decided to settle in Lubango. We have been moving back and forth for the last twenty years (Catarina, October 2015).

Catarina introduced herself to me as a Portuguese migrant but later other Portuguese migrants who knew Catarina shared the information that she was, actually, a white Angolan who used to live in Portugal. Nevertheless, the important aspect of Catarina's story is her capacity to live in two worlds, echoing what Smith (2006) called 'transnational lives' in the context of his research on Mexican-Americans. Catarina is able to navigate between Angola and Portugal and to present herself either as a Portuguese migrant – when the situation is convenient – or as a white Angolan. These groups are also divided by class: rich white Angolans and Angolans of mixed race are able to navigate easily between the two worlds. In some cases, they are able to invite relatives and friends struggling with unemployment in Portugal. The existence of white and mixed-race Angolans in postcolonial Angola raises the question of race not just with the renewed presence of Portuguese migrants but also within Angolan society more generally.

4.10 The question of race in postcolonial Angola

The existence of diverse racial minority groups in postcolonial Angola begs the question of how race has been managed there given the long history of Portuguese colonial racism. It is important to remember that, in some cases, postcolonial policies continue to indirectly reflect aspects of Portuguese colonialism, in particular when it comes to understanding racism.

As mentioned earlier, race became one of the key topics in the MPLA leadership before and after the end of Portuguese colonialism. One of the reasons for this was the dominance of white and mixed-race Angolans in key positions of the structure of the MPLA. For those Angolans who experienced oppression and humiliation under the Portuguese colonial system, the MPLA leadership represented the old colonial regime (da Cruz 2019). The resultant dispute was not only about the representation of black faces within the structure of the MPLA; it was also prominent in matters of language and cultural etiquette (Moco 2015). It created a particular myth of Angola that did not represent the reality of the majority. Therefore, it is fair to say that the postcolonial government of the MPLA inherited a country that was ideologically, ethnically and racially divided and polarised. The polarisation characteristic of postcolonial Angola called for the need to create another myth that accommodates and unites different groups together. However, the perceived dominance of white and mixed-race Angolans within the MPLA leadership became a huge setback. Much of the problem ignited from the perceived privilege which selected groups of Angolans had during Portuguese colonialism and continued to enjoy under the new postcolonial dispensation (Schubert 2017). For some Angolans within the MPLA, the dominance of white and mixed-race Angolans was perceived as a continuation of the old colonial order. According to da Cruz (2019), two different positions developed from these disputes within the MPLA leadership that had a significant impact on how race, language and identity are understood in postcolonial Angola.

The first position advocated a more radical approach, arguing that, given the historical privilege of white and mixed-race Angolans under colonialism, their influence and representation within the MPLA should be reduced in order to re-address the legacy of the Portuguese colonial system. Those arguing for a reduction of the said privileged groups wanted a better representation of black Angolans in leadership positions in the MPLA. One can argue that this debate was more about power struggles within the MPLA than race although da Cruz (2019) insists that race was a key element. The radical group wanted a clean break with the old Portuguese colonial order, which they perceived as hegemonic within postcolonial Angola's new dispensation. Da Cruz argues that these disputes terminated with the massacre – known as the 27 May 1977 massacre – during which members of the radical wing of the MPLA, accused of trying to overthrow the MPLA government, were purged.[44] The second position argues that race was not that important in the new Angola. White and mixed-race Angolans had positions of leadership within the MPLA based on their skills and competence rather than on the colour of their skin (da Cruz 2019). The discourse of 'skilled white bodies' became associated with being white in Angola, as this thesis will demonstrate in the next chapter. The disputes between these two groups culminated in a political purge of the radical wing of the party. Thus, moderate members of the MPLA – mainly those who did not see the importance of race in postcolonial Angola – won the debate and their victory paved the way for two important realities.

---

44 There is a host of literature about the 27 May massacre. A radical position on race has been one of the theories that has been pushed while others believe that the disputes were more political, with one side claiming to be more Marxist than the other (Pawson 2014). However, da Cruz (2019) strongly argues that race played a significant role, since some members accepted the influence of white and mixed-race Angolans while others strongly contested it.

The first reality is that talking openly about race and questioning the existence of racism in postcolonial Angola became taboo. In other words, everyone seemed to know that some form of racism occurs from time to time but discussing it in public was more or less forbidden (da Cruz 2019). Secondly, Angola witnessed the reinforcement of the non-racial myth which was not unlike that of 'old' Lusotropicalism in Brazil, with particular emphasis on the myth of common descent (Schubert 2017). As a result of this, racism in Angola came to be understood as a problem of other countries, especially nearby South Africa and Namibia.[45] Moreover, given the end of the Portuguese colonial era, the question of racism came to be perceived as an old colonial problem that magically disappeared after the Angolan revolution.[46] In other words, racism was seen as a thing of the past that left Angola with the mass exodus of the colonisers. Following the exodus of the *retornados*, it was thought that there were not enough white people to speak of racism and the priority was to unite the country. Thus, it was argued, there was no point in bringing up an emotional subject that was no longer relevant in the new dispensation. These disputes frame the philosophical roadmap of Angolan racial relations with direct and indirect racial dynamics from Portugal and Brazil through the adopted myth of Lusotropicalism. The focus was to create a myth that includes every Angolan through the notion of common descent. According to Moco (2015), the postcolonial government discursively erased all ethnic and racial differences and reconstructed a myth of common descent as a key pillar of postcolonial society.

4.11 The myth of common descent in postcolonial Angola

Once the question of race and the role of white Angolans and mixed-race minorities was politically settled, at least within the MPLA leadership, the next step was to implement the myth of common descent that includes all

---

45 In the context of Cold War propaganda, South Africa was viewed as attempting to invade Angola in order to implement a similar racist regime to that of Namibia under South-African apartheid occupation.

46 Sawyer (2006) conducted a study dealing with race in post-revolution Cuba and concluded that race was assumed to be a problem of the past, with the Cuban revolution magically ending the old racialised structures and stratification. Although that was the case in theory, in practice race continues to dominate Cuban society and the social advances and educational integration of Afro-Cubans has not necessarily eliminated racial stratification (Sawyer 2006).

Angolans, irrespective of race or ethnicity. In theory the myth of common descent was part of the new socialist agenda of creating a united country devoid of any class, racial and linguistic differences. Racial divisions, hierarchies and networks inherited from the colonial era were dismissed (Schubert 2017). The notion of multiculturalism was shunned and the vision was to unite everyone under a single Angolan (but, actually, culturally Portuguese) identity. Unlike in post-apartheid South Africa, where differences were celebrated under the myth of the rainbow nation, differences in Angola were erased under the myth of creating 'new men' (*sic*). Those who insisted on having unity in difference were accused of promoting disunity and tribalism. Racism and ethnic particularities were seen as signs of obscurantism (Moco 2015). Under the myth of creating the 'new men', the Angolan postcolonial government pragmatically advocated for the rejection of differences (Schubert 2017). Difference was perceived as an attempt to divide the country. In some senses, the postcolonial Angolan government's position is similar to current migration debates in Northern European countries concerning the role of multiculturalism and, in particular, the growing emphasis on an assimilationist discourse (Vertovec and Wessendorf 2010). Migrants are expected to assimilate through programmes such as cultural and linguistic courses which, in some cases, are designed to encourage migrants to reject some of their cultural distinctiveness, like the use of headscarves (Bodemann and Yurdakul 2006). In the case of postcolonial Angola, there was a similar attempt at bringing different groups under a singular and homogenous identity constructed by the state and a rejection of cultural distinctiveness, especially 'African' distinctiveness, for the sake of national unity (Schubert 2017). This was done, however, without taking into consideration the diversity of Angola. In other words, there was a construction of a particular cultural/national identity that demanded certain forms of behaviour and belonging, in order to be part of the shared root that the state promotes. Among many other approaches, two ways stand out as instrumental in the promotion of the myth of common descent by the state: the first is the Angolan national anthem and the second is through popular discourse.

First, the Angolan national anthem clearly depicts the myth of common descent by evoking the topic of unity, as the chorus here shows:

Forward Angola!
Revolution through the Power of the People!
A United Country, Freedom,
One People, one Nation!

The concept of *one people and one nation* demonstrates the unity that the postcolonial government wanted to forge. However, closer scrutiny indicates that this unity is based on certain criteria borrowed from Portuguese colonialism, as already mentioned, such as the Portuguese language and names. At the heart of the myth is the dismissal of race and ethnicity as irrelevant in the new dispensation without providing the necessary means to address the colonial legacy. When one pays attention to the lived realities in Angola, one is faced with evident paradoxes, as the country hosts various forms of discrimination against different sections of Angolan society (Moco 2015). In other words, there was no total break with the old Portuguese colonial order in terms of uniting the country.

The second way was the popularisation of the myth through popular culture such as those observed in political slogans. The idea was to see Angola as a united entity devoid of any racial and ethnic discrimination. Da Cruz (2019) quotes one popular song that was sung by the famous Angolan singer Teta Landu, which demonstrates the dominant discourse on race in postcolonial Angola. The song can loosely be translated from Portuguese to English as follows:

> *Angola move forward. Your path is only one. This path ahead is difficult, but happiness will come later, this path ahead is difficult. But freedom will come later, Angola move forward, your path is only one. If you are white it does not matter to anyone. If you are mixed race it does not matter to anyone. If you are black it does not matter to anyone. But what really matters is your willingness to make Angola better and an Angola truly free and independent.*

There are two important points that this popular postcolonial song makes. The first is the recognition of the diversity of postcolonial Angola; that Angola is for everyone. Second, the song uses a Lusotropicalist discourse of non-racism and directly dismisses the importance of race and social hierarchies inherited from Portuguese colonialism. Here, emphasis is put on the importance of the willingness of all Angolans to unite and work for a common good. The song might also be seen as a response to the growing discontent of some members of Angolan society who saw postcolonial Angola as racially stratified (da Cruz 2019).

As mentioned before, the failure to deal with the issue of race created a society which, on the surface, appears racially integrated but which, in reality, is still racially divided. In certain sectors of the Angolan labour market, in particular in Lubango, the over-representation of white and mixed-race Angolans is very visible. As Alfredo, in Lubango, put it:

Angolan whites and Angolans of mixed race generally have good relation-ships with black Angolans. Here it is not like in Namibia or South Africa, where there is always this tension. Here we can socialise together, even inter-marry if you have enough money. But when it comes to offering employment opportunities, especially in the private sector here in Lubango, they just work among themselves. When the private banks opened, they hired only whites and people of mixed race to work there. You could find one or two black per-sons but the majority in management are whites and mixed race. When one questions why this was the case, one gets automatically accused of being racist for asking, or accused of trying to cause trouble (Alfredo, Lubango, September 2015).

There are some important points raised by Alfredo that are worth noting. First, Alfredo recognises the existence of cordial relationships between different Angolans, probably in comparison to his own experience of Namibia and South Africa, where racial divisions are obvious. He then points out that interracial marriage between different groups can happen once a black person has enough money. This draws on the Angolan popular myth that interracial marriage between black and white Angolans only happens when a black person is rich. Even though he used the myth, he also mentions that upward social mobility is a necessary condition for a black Angolan to integrate and be considered good enough for intermarriage. So, one has to be economically well off to be accepted, according to the myth. This simply means that white and mixed-race Angolans, on the surface, appear to have relatively amicable relationships with black Angolans without obvious boundaries – it does *not* mean that racial stratifications do not exist. Second, Alfredo acknowledges the existence of racial stratification in certain workplaces in Lubango which are dominated by white Angolans and those of mixed race. Here again, Alfredo might be echoing the Portuguese colonial division of labour that allocates certain tasks to certain groups, confining black Angolans to physical labour and allocating whites to managerial and administrative roles. Nowadays, these dynamics are hidden behind dominant Angolan discourses of 'competent', skilled whites versus 'incompetent' and unskilled black Angolans. Maria, a white Angolan manager, echoed this:

Angolans are incompetent. That is why we have Portuguese migrants. I have many Angolan graduates who come to me looking for jobs but I do not em-ploy them, because they are incompetent. Maybe I employ those who studied outside of Angola but those Angolans who studied here in Angola are not good for employment (Maria, Lubango, August 2015).

Maria was, technically, speaking about Angolans in general but, in reality, she would be referring to black Angolans because the company where she is a manager is predominantly staffed by white and mixed-race Angolans. Yet, it is questionable whether the dominance of white and mixed-race Angolans is due to competence alone or is the result of long-established racialised networks of families and friends that operate in Lubango. Portes (1998) points out how such long-established racialised networks could function as a form of social capital that helps to selectively provide employment opportunities for a particular racial or ethnic group and can also monopolise certain business sectors. It is not far-fetched to argue that, in the case of Lubango, racialised networks function, in some cases, as a type of social capital that provides opportunities for both white and mixed-race Angolans.

Third, Alfredo points out that, in Lubango, those who dare to challenge the perceived racial stratification of the private sector are blamed for being racist. Alfredo's opinion about such accusations is reflected here in Maria's comment about racism in Angola. She reflects her unease with conversations about racism saying: *'Angolans now want to talk about racism like we live in America. We are a tiny minority – you cannot speak of racism like in America; we are all living peacefully here'*. In other words, as in Brazil and Portugal, in Lubango there is denial of the existence of racism. Racism is something that is perceived as being 'foreign'. This confirms da Cruz's (2019) argument that, in postcolonial Angola, race is a taboo topic that most people prefer to turn a blind eye to and rationalise with a discourse of skills and competence. In other words, the indirect message that this attitude is sending out is that white Angolans are competent and black Angolans are not (some of these dynamics will be developed further in Chapter Five when dealing with coloniality). The next section demonstrates more concretely the persistence of racial stratification in postcolonial Angola.

4.12 The taboo of semi-stratified postcolonial Angola

The topic of racial stratification in postcolonial Angola has been discussed before the recent Portuguese migration to Angola. Malaquias (2000) has argued that certain sectors of the postcolonial Angolan economy were racially stratified, in particular the private sector, which is dominated by white and mixed-race Angolans. Krug (2011), however, criticised Malaquias' (2000) stance on Angolan postcolonial racial stratification on the basis that no statistical evidence is provided for this claim. Malaquias was probably referring to a variety of general observations, sentiments and discourses surrounding black Angolans. When it comes to contemporary Angola and its experience with Portuguese immigrants, Alfredo's recollections, as well as my own extensive observations, indicate that some sectors of Lubango's economy are still stratified. This stratification is not peculiar to Lubango, being also observed in other places where there is a minority of white Angolans and Angolans of mixed race. Da Cruz (2019) argues that such stratification is the result of the failure of the MPLA to deal with the race issue, coupled with the lack of genuine ideological commitment to equality able to tackle centuries of racism. In Lubango and elsewhere, there is a visible stratification of white Angolans and Angolans of mixed-race in some private sectors. As Daniel, a black Angolan who has a business in the construction sector in Lubango put it:

> *If you have a business here in Lubango and you can afford to have a white person as a manager, it is better. The banks and clients take your business seriously once you have a white person as a manager; sometimes I prefer my white manager to deal with banks because they trust him more than me – the owner of the business* (Daniel, Lubango, October 2015).

In other words, postcolonial Angola still holds on to the myth that things only work well if a white person is or is seen to be in charge, even if they are not – as in Daniel's final remark. One explanation for this predicament might be rooted in Portuguese colonial Afro-pessimistic attitudes and embodied postcolonial assimilates who continue to hold similar views (Soares de Oliveira 2015). Similarly, Åkesson (2016) pointed out that behind every rich Angolan there is a white manager and consultant. The justification for these incongruences is camouflaged under the discourse of the lack of a skilled and competent workforce, as Maria reiterated in the previous section. It is nigh on impossible to understand this current condition without taking into account the long Portuguese colonial legacy.

The question that remains to be asked is whether such stratification was deliberately designed or whether it happened by accident. The typical response to this always boils down to competence and skills. However, participants like Alfredo tend to view this stratification as a latent racism that allows well-established networks to operate unchallenged:

> *White Angolans and Angolans of mixed race only offer opportunities among themselves; you might have one or two black persons just for show but the big bosses are always white or mixed race. Do you remember when we used to have those automobile races during the festivities of Lubango in the '80s?*

Those days there were only one or two blacks participating in those automobile car races – the rest were all white Angolans and Angolans of mixed race. Today is even worse, just look at some companies (Alfredo, Lubango, September 2015).

Here, Alfredo is concerned not just with networks but with something that he believes has been there in Lubango before the more-recent Portuguese migration. According to him, Lubango has always been a semi-segregated place. Under Portuguese colonial rule, Lubango was one of the few places in Angola that had majority white and mixed-race populations. This colonial legacy seems to continue to operate in the form of strong networks. Schubert (2017) argues that the problem is not only related to existing networks among white Angolans, Angolans of mixed race and black assimilates but also to the fact that postcolonial Angola had, in many cases, inherited Portuguese colonial racial hierarchies that unconsciously manifest themselves in different situations. These racial hierarchies remained unquestionable. Questioning them is often interpreted as an attempt to disrupt social cohesion with foreign ideas of race that are not relevant to the Angolan context (da Cruz 2019).

It is worth noting that racial stratification is not only happening in spaces dominated by white and mixed-race Angolans – it is also indirectly encouraged by black assimilates who simply do not trust in the capacity of black Angolans and Africans in general (Soares de Oliveira 2015). Racial stratification in Angola is not limited to employment in the private sector but also extends to certain public places like restaurants and night clubs, which seem to be reserved for white, mixed-race and a few selected black Angolans (da Cruz 2019; Schubert 2017). There is no single visible sign in Angola that prohibits black Angolans from entering certain places but there are other mechanisms to make sure that, in certain gatherings, black attendance is limited. This is done through dress code, price hikes and special reservations.[47] The counter-argument to this is that race does not play a role in Angolan society at all – instead, class does. There are indeed intersections between race and class in Lubango, where there is a strong associa-

---

47 There was a case of an Angolan human-rights activist who was removed from a restaurant predominantly frequented by white and mixed-race Angolans and some white foreigners in Luanda (da Cruz 2019). Da Cruz points out that incidents like this have become common in Angola but that there are always black Angolans defending some of these actions with 'explanations' like 'The person was discriminated against because he did not dress properly or because it was a misunderstanding'.

tion of whiteness and mixed race with wealth and a comfortable, even lux-urious, lifestyle of consumerism and materialism. This is evident in one of Angola's slang terms, *vida mulata*. The literal translation of *vida mulata* is a 'mixed-race life' but the meaning in this context is related to wealth and the good life. In other words, being white and mixed race in postcolonial Angola is synonymous with a particular lifestyle associated with power, prestige and material wealth.

4.13 *Conclusion*

Portuguese migration to Angola is intrinsically linked to Portuguese colonialism. It is almost impossible to understand the Portuguese migration of the 2000s and 2010s to Angola without understanding the historical, cultural, political and social networks that link these countries together. In light of this, Chapter 4 has presented the historical legacy of Lusotropicalism by looking at its roots in Brazil through the work of Freyre (1946, 1961). The argument here is that Freyre's ideas not only influenced Brazil and Portugal but also postcolonial Angola. The Lusotropicalism thesis not only focused on Portuguese colonialism in Brazil but also extended to Portuguese colonies in Africa and Asia, to serve as flawed evidence of a supposedly benevolent Portuguese colonial system. Furthermore, Freyre's ideas indirectly continue to dominate these three countries, even in postcolonial times, especially when it comes to race relations and the myth of a non-racial society.

Lusotropicalism was adopted as an official ideology and propaganda of the Portuguese colonial system to defend the continuation of Portuguese colonialism in Africa and it was presented as a tool that had helped to bring civilisation to black Africans. However, in spite of its claims, Lusotropicalism did not reflect the reality of Portuguese colonialism. It ignored the atrocities of the Portuguese colonial system and selectively focused on other aspects which presented this system in a positive light. In other words, Lusotropicalism was selective in reading and understating the multifaceted power of Portuguese colonialism and it ignored the brutal system of forced labour and social apartheid. Although Lusotropicalism has been dismissed as a myth, some of its central ideas continue to dominate Portugal and its previous colonies such as Angola. Postcolonial Angola still perpetuates Lusotropicalism by reinventing it as a myth of common descent for which the usage of the Portuguese language and personal names is as central as it was in colonial times. These discourses are used to construct the imaginary of what it means to be a true Angolan who transcends and ignores racial, ethnic, linguistic and class differences. Therefore, this sort of neo-Lusotropicalism and its claims of a benevolent postcolonial imaginary continue to operate in contemporary Angola and are pertinent to our understanding of recent migration from Portugal and how this is shaping or reproducing old colonial relations.

Chapter 5: The coloniality of power and Portuguese migration to Angola

5.1 Introduction

The previous chapter concentrated on some of the Portuguese colonial legacies in Angola, with particular emphasis on the development of the myth of Lusotropicalism as well as its impact on race relations in Portugal and postcolonial Angola. This chapter, parts of which draw on a recently published paper (Augusto and King 2020), analyses aspects of both the coloniality of power – including symbolic power – and the consequent advantages that Portuguese migrants have in Angola by virtue of being European. The coloniality of power hierarchises people based on their geographical, racial and cultural provenance and characteristics. As such, any positive traits are attributed to Portuguese migrants and negative traits to local Angolans. Under the coloniality of power, white Portuguese migrants in Angola are given certain privileges that are based not only on their skills but also on their admired European identity. These privileges and advantages often masquerade as the discourse of 'highly skilled' Portuguese migration to Angola and the culture of the 'work ethic' in contrast to the 'lazy native' Angolan. In this light, the chapter looks empirically at the coloniality of power, the consequences of Portuguese migrant privileges and the latent conflicts which develop in response to this notion of Portuguese privilege. It is important to note that the chapter does not negate the tangible contributions of Portuguese migrants in Angola. Rather, it highlights the complexities and ambiguities of 'skill' as a result of the uneven geographies of power, privilege and colonial history between Angola and Portugal. The differences in development and in what I call 'ethnic capital' allow semi-skilled and unskilled Portuguese migrants to be considered as skilled in a country like Angola. These factors and others are empirically discussed and analysed in this chapter.

5.2 The ethnic capital of Portuguese migrants in Angola

I met Abel at his house after one of the participants told me about an Angolan consultant who worked with Portuguese migrants. Abel spent part of his life studying and working in Brazil and returned to Lubango after completing his PhD in agriculture. He also trained as a project manager and followed a computer course in Brazil. He taught for more than 13 years at a local university in Lubango, as well as offering basic computer courses at a private school there. Because of his impeccable curriculum, Abel worked on various development projects with Portuguese migrants. I was interested in interviewing him because of his fascinating academic background as well as his experience of working abroad and with Portuguese migrants. Moreover, given the dominant discourse that Portuguese migrants are employable in Angola because of their skills, it was important to find a skilled Angolan with experience in various sectors to see if there were certain differences in working conditions and why. The story of Abel helps us to understand how the coloniality of power operates in Angola, in particular when it comes to differences in salaries and working conditions between skilled Angolans and Portuguese migrants, both doing the same work.

In a previous interview, Maria argued that Angolans trained outside the country and having some work experience are better prepared for employment than Angolans trained in Angola. However, listening to skilled Angolans like Abel, it became clear that, in some cases, this dichotomy is artificial because the plight of both categories of Angolans is similar, as Abel's story will demonstrate.[48] Moreover, the division between Angolans trained abroad and those trained in Angola is made because the former are few in number and, when available, seem to come from the political and economic elite or are white and mixed-race Angolans. The plight of the two categories is very visible when one listens to complaints about the salaries and working conditions of Angolans trained abroad in comparison to Portuguese migrants. Although Abel should technically be considered as a highly skilled Angolan, when I asked him if he had the same salary and working conditions as his Portuguese migrant colleagues he stated that, actually, there is a significant gap.

---

48 Moreover, an interesting aspect of the dichotomy of Angolans trained within Angola and Angolans trained abroad is that, in some cases, the latter belong to the Angolan political elite (Soares de Oliveira 2015). In the case of Lubango there is an association between studying abroad and race and class; studying abroad is something that is expected to be limited to the black elite and white and mixed-race Angolans. In other words, there is an intersection between race, class and power in access to different pathways through higher education.

I worked with Portuguese migrants on various projects. One of the projects that I used to work on, my boss was less qualified and less skilled than me. She only had a Bachelor's degree and a few years of work experience in comparison to me. To make matters worse, she did not know much about the project [on malaria prevention]. *Technically, I had to do most of the work because it was the first time she had worked on malaria prevention. Nevertheless, she was appointed as senior manager and got paid twice as much as I did. Besides her salary, her accommodation was paid for and her transport was covered. She was also allowed to visit Portugal twice a year. This is just one of the many examples that are happening here. You look around and you think that everyone who comes here under the umbrella of 'skilled' is skilled in some way; however, it is bit more complex than that. At first, it really bothered me – she was not incompetent but she did not have a clue about malaria prevention. We never had any conflict for the two years that we worked together, but I did most of the work because she gave me the freedom to run the project. However, the truth is that she was paid more because of where she came from. Here in Angola, skills are not enough – people think that, if you come from Europe, you know everything and deserve to be treated as special* (Abel, Lubango, September 2015).

The experience of Abel demonstrates three important aspects of the coloniality of power. The first is that skilled Angolans do not earn as much as Portuguese migrants and such discrepancy in salary and working conditions is not always related to skill but to the uneven geography of privilege and colonial history between Portugal and Angola. European 'ethnic capital' plays a significant role in assessing how much a person should be paid. In other words, being white and a Portuguese migrant in Angola is an asset that earns special treatment, in some cases based on coloniality. Second, Abel's case demonstrates that, while African migrants moving to European countries find themselves on the lower strata of the socio-economic ladder, often doing jobs which are beneath their skill and qualifications level, Portuguese migrants, regardless of their skill level, always start towards the top. The coloniality of power gives a certain ethnic capital to Europeans, enabling them to navigate to a vantage position in spaces which they had previously colonised. However, the same cannot be said of colonised Africans moving to European spaces, where they find themselves at the bottom of the socio-economic ladder, a position which can endure for several generations. There is an imbalance of power, with one group having symbolic power and advantage over the other. Thirdly, the case of Abel is not unique to Lubango; other studies, cited below, have indicated how the coloniality of power operates when Europeans move to their former colonial spaces.

Armbruster's (2010) work on German migrants in Namibia seems to indicate similar patterns of ethnic capital, as does Andrucki's (2017) study on white Europeans in South Africa. Given the uneven geography of power relations between Europe and the rest of the colonised countries, in particular in Africa, the coloniality of power places excessive trust in the capacity and ability of Europeans, even in cases where they are not qualified. Although Abel deserves to be paid a salary which is similar to or higher than that of his less-skilled Portuguese migrant colleague, the coloniality of power and the geography of uneven development between Angola and Portugal dictate otherwise.[49] The official justification for this anomaly continues to be that Portuguese migrants are 'expatriates' who deserve to be paid different salaries because they are bringing in the unique skills needed for the economic development of Angola.[50] They also need to be offered salaries which are at least commensurate with what they could earn in Portugal, otherwise they would have no incentive to move. Moreover, Angolans working with Portuguese migrants are then able to gain work experience and a better work ethic once the latter leave Angola. However, this discourse does not reflect the reality on the ground, as there is no indication that every Portuguese migrant in Angola is skilled or that skills are being transferred to Angolans. In some cases, as Abel indicated, it is the Portuguese migrants who are learning on the job and there is in effect an interchange of knowledge. A good example is the case of Fernando, a Portuguese migrant who works as a mechanic at a construction company in Lubango and who testified as follows:

---

49 It is difficult to calculate the difference in salaries between Portuguese migrants and skilled Angolans, as no Portuguese migrant was willing to reveal the exact amount of his or her salary. Some gave an estimate – at the time that this research was conducted, some Portuguese migrants were earning the equivalent of 4,000–6,000 euros per month, including housing benefit and a travel allowance to visit Portugal at least twice a year. It is important to mention that not every Portuguese migrant in Angola had the same working conditions and salaries. Each case was different. However, in comparison with Angolans there was a significant difference, as some Angolans at the time were earning 1,000–2,000 euros without other benefits.

50 This statement was shared by an Angolan embassy official at one of the presentations that I gave at the Brazilian Embassy in Berlin in December 2015 on the topic of the *Global South und Europa – Die Rolle der CPLP-Länder*. The official indirectly supported the discrepancy in salaries between Portuguese migrants and Angolans, claiming that Portuguese migrants in Angola were mostly skilled.

I must say that, when I first came here, I thought I would be able to be the boss. But after seven years here, I realised that being here is also about learning from Angolans. For example, in Portugal, if you need a car spare part, you just go to a shop and buy it but, in Lubango, I learned from Angolans to improvise because the shops do not sell some spare parts for cars. You must import them from Namibia, South Africa or Portugal and they take forever to arrive. So, in my job I learned from my Angolan colleagues to improvise. Angolan mechanics have the capacity to make things work. For a spare part that could cost lots of money, they always manage to improvise and fix it. I did not learn this in Portugal because there you just exchange but here you improvise. Thus, I cannot say that I know everything and that I am not learning from Angolans as well (Fernando, Lubango, October 2015).

In spite of notions of dependency and co-dependency and the complex exchange of skills, the coloniality of power continues to represent Portuguese migrants as agents of development and thus deserving better salaries. This nuanced exchange of ideas and skills is something that Fernando admitted is also happening in other sectors. However, there are other cases where attitudes of superiority impede such interaction, as the case of Jorge (an Angolan) indicates:

When my boss came from Portugal, after six months he brought someone else to work as a senior engineer. He was supposed to be in charge of electricity generation because our company does not depend on unreliable public electricity. However, after a few weeks it became clear that the Portuguese engineer did not know much about his job. But he would not listen to Angolans who have been working with these generators for some time. He kept on trying to do new experiments and the other Angolans were trying to warn him not to touch certain areas of the generators. But he never listened to them, maybe because he thought they did not know what they were talking about. He was trying to do things without consulting the Angolan team. Then he received three electric shocks in less than a month working at our company. He has stopped touching the generator now because his Angolan colleagues reported him to the manager. I had heard that he is an engineer and gets paid as one but the mistakes he makes are not those of an engineer. Some Angolan colleagues suspect that he used to be just an electrician in Portugal but, here, he is considered as an engineer (Jorge, Lubango, October 2015).

Jorge's story illustrates that, in some cases, Portuguese migrants do not necessarily listen to Angolans – maybe because the former assume that their coming from Portugal is a synonym for knowing it all – and such situations often lead to conflict. Jorge's story also indicates how the coloniality of power helps Portuguese migrants to upgrade their qualifications once they arrive in Angola due to their ethnic capital. Åkesson's (2018) work on Portuguese migrants in Luanda arrived at a similar conclusion. However, ethnic capital and advantage encourage forms of resistance which could be considered as latent conflict.

5.3 Latent conflicts between Portuguese migrants and Angolan nationals

The coloniality of power, especially with regard to the salary discrepancies evident in Abel's and Jorge's narratives, created a situation of latent conflict between Portuguese migrants and Angolans, as the latter clearly felt that some of the Portuguese were not performing as well as they were expected to, yet were paid more. This latent tension has been interpreted as unsolved colonial tension or what Åkesson (2016) refers to as 'turning the tables' and 'postcolonial score-settling'. The interviews I conducted with Angolans and Portuguese migrants reveal that the tension between the two groups is primarily focused on the advantages and privileges that Portuguese migrants enjoy in the workplace in Angola. Skilled Angolans jealously crave these advantages, specifically in cases where they feel that they are performing better than the Portuguese migrants and yet are paid far less. They see such privileges and advantages as being granted unfairly to Portuguese migrants based on the fact that they come from Europe and are white;[51] but this only added to the great respect which Angolans generally have for Portuguese migrants and Portugal as a country. This special treatment and admiration of Portuguese migrants by a sector of Angolan society, together with the differences in salary, seems to be one cause of the latent conflict, as Alfredo, a black Angolan, pointed out:

---

51 It is important to mention that the latent tension between skilled Angolans and Portuguese migrants sometimes carries a nationalistic and anticolonial sentiment. However, unlike in the northern countries where nationalistic and anticolonial sentiments are used for political mobilisation against migrants, in Angola, such sentiments do not have enough public support to politically mobilise against Portuguese migration. This could be explained by the presence of white and mixed-race Angolans, as mentioned before, but it could also be because there is no need to politically capitalise on Portuguese migrants. However, the same cannot be said of migrants in Angola from other African countries, who are often targeted by state-based violent discourses of security similar to those we hear about from northern countries (Schubert 2017; Soares de Oliveira 2015).

When you live outside Angola you experience all kinds of discrimination but you just train yourself to cope with it because it is not your country and you long for the day when you will go back and all this unfairness will stop. But then you come back to Angola and you see the same things you experienced outside of your country. You feel like speaking out but you cannot do that. If Angolans were to earn more than the Portuguese in Portugal just because they were coming from Angola, it would be a big scandal in Portugal but when that happens here, it is accepted as the most normal thing – Angolans even, some of them, think it is normal and okay (Alfredo, Lubango, September 2015).

The complaint voiced by Alfredo is common among Angolans who have been migrants before; they are somehow more conscious of their rights than Angolans who have never migrated. Claims of injustice in the workplace by these return migrants are sometimes interpreted by Portuguese migrants as racism against them, or as a kind of 'reverse racism', as demonstrated by Teresa, a Portuguese lecturer at a private university:

Generally, we get along well with most Angolans but there are other Angolans who are racist against us; they are always complaining about the Portuguese. We are here to work and help this country to develop but they are always saying that we are racist. Look, there are also many Angolans living in Portugal and claiming social benefits and the Portuguese do not make a big deal about it, because the Portuguese by nature are not racist – we are hospitable people. But you come here to work and help this country and some Angolans complain about you being racist and having it easy here. I know an Angolan who used to live and study in Lisbon. When she came back to Angola she started complaining about the Portuguese being racist and having an easy life here. I was so upset with her because I knew her in Lisbon. She even benefited from the Erasmus programme. Now she is going around claiming that the Portuguese have it easy here with their salary and their racism. We work hard for what we earn here. I have decided to un-friend her on Facebook for she is ungrateful. Yes, there are differences in salaries but that is not because of racism but because we have the skills and we are helping this country (Teresa, Lubango, September 2015).

Teresa seems to think that it is justifiable for Portuguese migrants to earn more than skilled Angolans because the former are helping to develop Angola, unlike Angolans in Lisbon who, according to her, are dependent on social benefits. Whether or not this is the case, questioning Portuguese migrants' privileges on the Angolan labour market creates a certain discomfort for them. In other words, some Portuguese migrants do not find it problematic at all that they have certain privileges and are paid more than Angolans. Waldorff's (2017) research on Portuguese migrants in Luanda alludes to similar dynamics of privilege and latent conflict as a result of the special treatment that Portuguese migrants receive in the workplace. Waldorff writes how one of his Angolan participants revealed that it was common to separate Angolans and Portuguese during meal times at the company canteen where he was working in Luanda. The Portuguese migrants were served different meals from the Angolans. Even in cases where they were doing the same job and working in the same office, they were separated at meal times. This seemingly insignificant gesture of soft apartheid often leads to resentment against Portuguese migrants, although this is expressed in private because of the fear of losing one's job. However, Pedroto , an Angolan lecturer at a private university in Lubango, openly voiced his resentment concerning what he perceived to be discrimination against Angolans in private universities in Angola:

I am not scared to speak out. You can record me if you wish, I do not care. Here, the Portuguese are treated like special people – you just have to compare my office and the office of my Portuguese colleagues. They have air conditioning and we do not, they have more space and we do not. We work together but we never meet because they are up there and we are down here. Some of them have transport and housing provided by the university; we have to pay for our own transport and housing. You can quote me, this is how things work here in Lubango. I am not against the Portuguese but I am against this special treatment. We are doing the same job here, which is lecturing, but they receive special treatment (Pedroto, Lubango, September 2015).

Some Portuguese migrants seem not to understand why there is resentment against them from those not given special treatment. On the contrary, some of the migrants are also victims of Angola's complex and bureaucratic system, as the next section demonstrates.

5.3.1 Portuguese migrants dealing with the Angolan bureaucratic system

Besides the latent conflict due to the apparent privileges that they have in comparison with skilled Angolans, Portuguese migrants have constantly pointed out that they are also discriminated against by the Angolan visa system, complaining that it is designed to make life difficult for them. Many have requested that the Angolan government make visa-processing easier for them. Sabina, a Portuguese migrant, recalled the struggles she had faced when applying for an Angolan visa and work permit. She explained that she first went there and worked illegally on an 'ordinary' or 'tourist' visa which was valid for three months – something which she confirmed was common practice among Portuguese migrants in Angola because the *visto de trabalho*, the work visa, was difficult to obtain and took longer. After that, she applied for another three months and then left Angola for Portugal in order to apply for a work permit. She stated that it took more than six months for her work visa to be granted so that she could return back to and work legally in Angola.

> *Most of these Portuguese migrants you see here have worked at least once on tourist visas; there are only a few here who came initially with a work permit – maybe those working for big companies who have insider contacts at the embassy to enable them to secure a visa. It is common practice to work on a tourist visa; everyone knows that it takes forever to obtain a work permit and it took me more than six months and lots of paperwork to get my one-year work permit. And it only lasts a year and then you have to apply again here in Angola and you need to have connections to get your visa renewed. It is not just about the paper; you must pay extra. In the Angolan consulate in Lisbon, if you have all the papers, it is not a problem. But here in Angola you always need to pay a gasosa.[52] Life is not always easy for Portuguese migrants in Angola* (Sabina, Lubango, September 2015).

According to Sabina, most Portuguese migrants who do not have the proper documentation feel vulnerable because they are afraid of being stopped by the police, an event which is often followed by the necessity to pay a bribe in order not to be arrested and potentially expelled from the country.

Sabina could be classified as a self-employed migrant who decided to come to Angola without the support of a company. However, there are other classes of Portuguese migrants, working for corporations or with members of the political and economic elite, who are recruited directly from Portugal through an agency. They are usually able to rely on their employers to take care of the work permit, which they either obtain through expensive private visa agencies or acquire through their political connections. These migrants have different experiences of the Angolan bureaucracy to Sabina's. A visit to an agency in Lisbon responsible for the recruitment of Portuguese migrants reveals a well-organised system that guarantees that migrants going to Angola have all the necessary bureau-

---

52 *Gasosa* literally means a fizzy drink but, in this context, it means a small bribe.

cratic and contract-related hurdles resolved. However, even some migrants with proper work documents have admitted that they have been stopped and harassed by the police before. It is well known in Angola that some policemen have a tendency to target white people (Åkesson and Orjuela 2019). My participants accused the Angolan authorities of discrimination in visa-processing, document-checking and driving offences (genuine or false), because they harbour colonial resentment, claims which need to be carefully evaluated and contextualised in the light of the coloniality of power and of being.

5.3.2 Analysing and contextualising claims of anti-Portuguese discrimination in light of the coloniality of power

Portuguese migrants may have significant power and privilege in the workplace but they can face obstacles outside it, which has led some to claim that they have been subject to acts of anti-Portuguese discrimination. There are four factors to be considered when analysing and contextualising claims of resentment against Portuguese migrants; all four are somehow related to the coloniality of power.

The first factor or claim is that the draconian Angolan visa process discriminates against Portuguese migrants, most of whom complain that they had problems with their visas, primarily due to the anti-Portuguese sentiments that dominate the Angolan migration office. However, the situation is not quite as clear-cut as that. While it is true that the visa process is indeed complex, it is also an opportunity for some officials to extort money from Portuguese and other migrants in general. However, speaking to Antonio, who is one of the officials responsible for processing visa applications in Lubango, revealed a different story:

> *We are just doing our job. I do not know how the Portuguese migration system works but I know that it is also not easy for Angolans to apply for visas to go to Portugal either. Some of these Portuguese migrants want to be treated like special people. If you ask for a document, sometimes they do not bring the right one because they think they can just get away with things. Some of them do not even want to wait in the queue like everyone else. They always want things to be done according to their plans and they try to tell you how we are supposed to do our job. The other day my colleague asked one Portuguese migrant to wait in the queue like everyone else because he walked in and found people in the queue and wanted to jump the queue, but my colleague told him to wait in line like everyone else. It is not discrim-*

ination to ask that; if the Mamadou *can wait, why can't the Portuguese wait as well? Why do we have to treat Portuguese migrants differently? We have rules and regulations that must apply to all foreigners* (Antonio, Lubango, October 2015).

Antonio's experience as a migration official indicates that the claims of discrimination against Portuguese migrants need to be properly contextualised. In some cases, Portuguese migrants might expect to be treated as special migrants because of their social status in the workplace. Moreover, Vala *et al.* (2008) point out that Angolan migrants in Portugal face similar scrutiny when applying for visas and may encounter diverse forms of discrimination whilst living there. Vradis, Papada, Painter and Papoutsi (2019) also point out how the draconian and homogenous visa requirements for migration into Europe are designed to make it almost impossible for migrants from developing countries to obtain visas. Portuguese migrants might not be aware that Angolans applying for visas to Portugal face similar or even-more-draconian visa requirements. The coloniality of power seems to blind Portuguese migrants, who see the rigid visa problems only from their advantageous European perspective rather than as a common practice that states use to limit the flow of migrants. The Angolan visa regime is indeed rigid, complex and, in some cases, corrupt, as indicated by Åkesson (2018). However, it is questionable whether this rigidity is limited to Portuguese migrants alone or is just the nature of the bureaucratic regime, as suggested by Antonio.

Secondly, we need to consider that Portuguese migrants' claims of discriminatory treatment may derive partly from the fact that their only other migration experience is likely to have been within Europe, where they enjoy free movement as EU citizens, with minimal bureaucratic hurdles. Here, again, the role of the coloniality of power plays a significant role in understating why it is hard for Portuguese migrants to obtain visas – they feel insecure and vulnerable once their EU member-states' bureaucratic visa privileges are stripped away in contexts like Angola, as Teresa stated:

We are here to work and help to develop this country and give more to this country than we take. They should make the visa process accessible to us – we are bringing in skills and they should not treat us like other foreigners. We speak the same language and we are brothers and sisters. Honestly some of these visa requirements are unnecessary. Look, I can go to Namibia and South Africa and stay there for three months with a tourist visa – no need to apply for a visa because I get it upon arrival. But here in Angola, where we have so much in common, it is hard for us to get a visa. These requirements are not good for business, which is why the tourism industry is dead here. Europeans prefer to go to Namibia and South Africa for tourism because those countries' visa systems make it easier for them to go there. Here, in order to apply for a tourism visa, you need to have an invitation letter, you pay a tourist visa fee and they ask for your criminal record and bank statements. All these requirements are only for a tourist visa – for a work permit it is even harder. It is like you are going to some advanced country but then you arrive here, you look around and there are lots of problems with basic needs. If they relaxed the visa requirements it would help this country's tourist industry. The landscape is very beautiful here and there is so much to explore but Europeans will never come here because of the visa requirements (Teresa, Lubango, September 2015).

Teresa's frustrations indicate that the Angolan visa regime is an impediment to the development of Angola because it does not permit the easy flow of migrants from Europe. In spite of her migration status, she still associates the European presence with the premise of development. Teresa also cites visa regimes in countries like Namibia and South Africa as examples for Angola to follow because, apparently, member-countries of the EU have the privilege of being able to go there without applying for visas, unlike in Angola.

Thirdly, we must contextualise the claim that, since most Portuguese migrants hold certain positions of power in their workplace, they expect the same power to be transferable in other spheres of Angolan society. As Antonio pointed out:

The Portuguese think they can be bosses everywhere in Angola; they are not used to listening to us. This is not the Angola of the '50s and '60s. Things have changed here and yet they think they can be the boss everywhere. So when they come for their visa renewal, they need to know who is in charge – you cannot be a boss everywhere (Antonio, Lubango, October 2015).

Antonio was delighted to share how some immigration officials use their bureaucratic powers to show Portuguese migrants who is in charge. More importantly, they demonstrate how the Portuguese coloniality of power is a limited concept when it comes to the draconian Angolan visa-application process. In other words, there is a power struggle between Angolan immigration officials and Portuguese migrants. This is probably one of the areas where Åkesson's (2016) concept of 'turning the tables' and 'postcolonial score-settling' might apply. Angolan immigration officials might be aware of the symbolic power that Portuguese migrants hold in their workplace and society in general and they try to reverse that in order to show who is in charge. Moreover, according to Åkesson (2016), this point-scoring is also an element of the mechanics of coloniality which does not fundamentally change the unequal relations between the two countries and two populations. Rather, it is a kind of symbolic protest.

The fourth factor affecting the analysis and contextualisation of claims concerns the complaints by Portuguese migrants that they are frequently targeted by corrupt police – it is common practice for the latter to request a bribe from visibly white Portuguese migrants driving in private cars. Although this might indeed be the case, nevertheless, acts of petty corruption or the expectation of a bribe by the police are common practice in everyday Angolan social life (Schubert 2017). Every Angolan driving a 'normal car', regardless of the colour of his or her skin, has been harassed at least once for a bribe by the police. However, there are exceptions to the rule: those driving expensive cars, government cars and business corporation cars with special number plates are rarely harassed because they are directly or indirectly associated with the political and economic elite. In other words, when dealing with everyday petty corruption in Angola, it is important not to lose sight of the class element associated with police harassment. Portuguese migrants might assume that they are targeted for being white. This might indeed be the case, in particular for the visa renewal process in Angola, as stated by Sabina. The question here is not whether the claims of police harassment and corrupt immigration officials are true or not but how to contextualise them within the wide spectrum of petty corruption in Angola. Portuguese migrants might indeed suffer from police harassment but the evidence seems to suggest that the situation is more complex – petty corruption would seem to be part and parcel of Angolan society (Schubert 2017; Soares de Oliveira 2015). What seems to be the reason why Portuguese migrants are harassed is the association of whiteness with being rich and the increased visibility of Portuguese migrants in Lubango. Some policemen might think that Portuguese migrants have plenty of money and may even be working in Angola illegally, a factor that could spur the police into harassing them. Rosalia, a white Angolan, stated that:

> *Before we had an increase of Portuguese migrants here in Lubango it was uncommon for the police to stop us but these days it looks like they are going after everyone who is white because they think we are all Portuguese migrants and that we are here illegally. The police are constantly asking for documents and* gasosa *from whites but let us not forget that it happens to everyone. If you work on a* kandongueiro *[a minibus used for public transport], probably the experience is worse because the police stop kan-*

dongueiro *workers more than anyone else* (Rosalia, Lubango, October 2015).

Therefore, when analysing the claims of racism towards Portuguese migrants in Angola, these four factors need to be considered. Having made these analyses, it is important to reiterate that this does not necessarily mean that some claims of discrimination against Portuguese migrants are not genuine. There are cases where Portuguese migrants *are* discriminated against, based on their nationality or their purchasing power. Fernando wanted to buy a house in Lubango but was refused because he was a Portuguese migrant:

> *I came here to work and, after I had settled down, my wife joined me and she also found a job here. We love it here in Lubango and we wanted to buy a house and start a family here because it is practical for us. There is also a Portuguese school but we were told that Portuguese nationals are not allowed to buy property in Angola. To own property, one needs to have Angolan nationality, which I consider unfair. In Portugal, everyone, regardless of their nationality, can buy a house. Most of the rich Angolans have houses in Portugal in places like Cascais and other posh areas in Portugal. Why are we not allowed to buy houses here?* (Fernando, Lubango, October 2015).

Fernando's experience demonstrates that, in some cases, Portuguese migrants suffer a sort of discrimination that forbids them from buying property in Angola. Further consultation with government official Antonio confirmed that property laws in Angola do, indeed, discriminate against Portuguese migrants as well as against other foreign nationals. Antonio also stated that although, in theory, the law forbids Portuguese migrants from buying property, there are ways to get around this:

> *Portuguese migrants and other foreigners are not allowed to buy property here, but there is a way around it. Those migrants married to Angolans can buy property in the name of the spouse. Those who apply for citizenship are also allowed to buy* (Antonio, Lubango, October 2015).

Portuguese migrants are probably not aware that some of the unconventional and protectionist Angolan laws apply to other foreigners as well.

5.4 The coloniality of power and being: situational skills in uneven geographies

Despite claims of discrimination against Portuguese migrants, coloniality plays a significant role in conferring Portuguese migrants in Angola with a special status when it comes to work and skills, as Abel pointed out earlier in this chapter. In the context of Angola, highly skilled Portuguese migration has only been vaguely defined and is open to diverse interpretations. Some Portuguese scholars of migration assume that this flow to Angola is predominantly one of skilled migration. According to David, a Portuguese migration expert in Lisbon,

> *I do not know the numbers of Portuguese migrants going to Angola but I assume that Portuguese migration to Angola is predominantly by skilled Portuguese and […] also linked to companies working in Angola* (David, Lisbon, July 2016).

Although David's analysis could well be partially correct, the skilled nature of Portuguese migrants in Angola is ambiguous. Sometimes there is no clear definition of who should be considered skilled. For example, is a Portuguese hairdresser or a migrant truck-driver for a mining company to be considered highly skilled? It appears that there is no clear definition of what it means to be highly skilled when it comes to Portuguese migrants in Angola.[53] However, due to geographical disparities in development, differences in the nature of the two labour markets and the inherited racist prejudices relating to Lusotropicalism and the coloniality of power, someone who is evaluated as highly skilled in Angola might not be considered so in Portugal. One country is considered to be developed, politically stable and linked to the strong economies of Europe; the other is seen as part of an underdeveloped Africa, battling to recover from decades of civil war and extreme inequality. These imagined geographies of a country's position within global political-economic hierarchies make the definition of 'skill' a complex and contextual matter. Portuguese migrants in Angola, regardless of their qualifications, are automatically considered skilled because they move from the so-called First World to the so-called Third World. Åkesson's (2018) research demonstrates how many of the Portuguese migrants in Luanda have questionable qualifications yet operate under the umbrella of 'skilled' labour, a status that they do not have in Portugal.

Portuguese migrants in Angola are aware of these hierarchies and try to profit from their advantageous position. This happens in two ways. First, jobs which would not normally be classified as highly skilled would be cat-

---

53 In studies of labour-market classification generally, divisions between highly skilled and skilled, lower-skilled and unskilled are problematic and ambiguous (Favell, Feldblum and Smith 2009).

egorised thus if a Portuguese worker was doing the job. Sabina, a Portuguese migrant who works in a beauty salon, is classified as a skilled migrant, even though there are several other locally run beauty salons in Lubango providing the same service. Interestingly enough, she is able to attract Angolan clients even though she charges more than the Angolan beauty salons because it is considered prestigious to go to a beauty salon run by a Portuguese migrant. Second, it is common to find Portuguese migrants working in jobs classified as highly skilled without fulfilling the normal requirements for such a job. One of the Portuguese migrants, Teresa, works as a lecturer at a private university in Lubango in spite of only having a Bachelor's degree qualification. When asked how she managed to obtain such a position, she responded by saying:

In Portugal I used to work as a high-school teacher. Here, I worked as a university lecturer. Yes, I only have a Bachelor's degree but it is different to have a Bachelor's degree in Angola and Portugal. The Portuguese educational system is far better and more demanding than the Angolan one. A student with a Bachelor's degree in Portugal is the equivalent to a Master's or more [in Angola]. The standards in Portugal are higher in comparison to those in Angola. I can see that from some of my Angolan colleagues. Here, some of them have a Master's degree but they cannot even write in Portuguese properly. That is why it makes sense for me to work as a lecturer here with a Bachelor's degree: because of the difference in the two systems. One is advanced and more demanding and the other is not (Teresa, Lubango, September 2015).

Teresa's experience is potentially applicable in other sectors too. In this case, normally, the expectation at university level in Angola would be that at least a Master's degree is required while, in Portugal and the rest of Europe, a doctorate would be the norm. However, in this case, the coloniality of power and the differential and uneven considerations of university 'quality' put the Portuguese migrant with a Bachelor's degree in the position of an Angolan with a Master's – in other words, differences in economic and historical development situate Portuguese migrants in an advantageous position. Teresa's statement perfectly illustrates what Hayes (2014) calls 'geographic arbitrage', whereby individuals with economic and symbolic status move across borders to take advantage of better opportunities in a particular transnational social field corresponding to a postcolonial, globalised division of labour. Initially applied by Hayes to North American retirees who moved to Ecuador to take advantage of the much lower costs of living, in a later paper Hayes and Pérez-Gañán (2017) applied the same 'geoarbitrage' principle to a case which is more similar to Portuguese migration to Angola – Spanish skilled labour migrants relocating to Ecuador to escape the Spanish economic crisis.

In both the Spain–Ecuador and Portugal–Angola cases of North-South migration, we see the same processes at work. The relative ease with which migrants from the global North can move to the global South enables both more- and less-skilled workers whose professional and personal livelihoods have been stifled by the economic crisis in Europe to access better career and income opportunities abroad. Although for both the Spanish and the Portuguese, northward migration to more prosperous European countries is an option, many see this as less professionally and personally attractive than the southward move, where they can benefit from the coloniality of power and being that procures them ethnic privileges (Hayes and Pérez-Gañán 2017: 124). The cultural and ethnic capital derived from being 'white' and coming from the centre of former colonial power gives them a symbolic advantage over locals. Klekowski von Koppenfels (2014) alludes to similar dynamics when she looks at American migrants in the UK, France and Germany and how these migrants, irrespective of their social and economic class, are treated better than migrants from other developing countries because they come from America. These dynamics can also extend to race. In an earlier study I argued that Angolan migrants in '90s Bavaria often projected themselves as African American soldiers stationed there – it was easier to be socially accepted as an African American soldier than an Angolan because the latter was associated with and stigmatised as being an asylum-seeker (Augusto 2012). On one level both groups were blacks but one group was socially accepted and tolerated while the other was rejected. In other words, the global geographic, economic and cultural hierarchy classifies people according to their country of origin; this is what Massey (1993) refers to as power geometry. African American soldiers in Bavaria had the privilege of being Americans; despite being black they were not like 'other' blacks from sub-Saharan Africa. In the case of Portuguese migrants in Angola, given the geographic positionality of Portugal as a member-country of the EU, Portuguese migrants have the luxury of being able to upgrade their skills once they arrive in a country like Angola. A Portuguese migrant in Angola is considered what Klekowski von Koppenfels (2014: 26) calls an *immigré deluxe* when referring to American migrants in Europe.

5.5 The coloniality of power and the marketing of 'white bodies'

The discourse on skills-based migration is not only limited to Portuguese migrants' advantages and privileges on the Angolan job market but also extends to how Portuguese and 'white bodies'[54] are perceived in Angola (Augusto and King 2020). Daniel had already pointed out how Angolan banks put more trust in companies with white-skinned managers than with black ones, while Alfredo critically pointed out how race operates within the job market in Lubango. These dynamics, however, extend to other spheres of Lubanga's social life, where 'white bodies' are represented as synonymous with success. As such, 'white bodies' are deployed, one might even say exploited, by some businesses in order to advance their business status. The marketing of whiteness refers to the practice that some business-owners and managers of middle-sized companies employ when they choose Portuguese migrants instead of black Angolans in order to present an image of a successful and stable enterprise. Tomas, who had studied and worked in Namibia, said he worked with Portuguese migrants before opening his own computer shop in Lubango. He pointed out that the employment of Portuguese migrants, in spite of their (by local standards) exorbitant salaries, should not be viewed solely as the result of Portuguese migrants' skills. For Tomas, there are other dynamics at work here:

Here in Lubango, people respect and admire Portuguese migrants. If you have a shop or any other business and you want to sell well, it is better that you employ a Portuguese migrant. Then the customers will believe that the products you are selling are genuine. You see, there are many fake goods sold here and they are all sold by langas *[migrants from the Democratic Republic of Congo] but having a white person in the front of the shop or as a manager helps. If you put a* langa *there, then people might think that the*

---

54 The concept of 'white bodies' has been significantly used in the social sciences in order to access inequality and the discrimination against minorities in the North. 'White bodies' is also related to 'white privilege', which is concerned with how whiteness offers certain advantages and opportunities in the labour market (Bhopal 2018; McIntosh 1989). This thesis uses 'white bodies' in a similar way to how Andrucki (2017) used it to assess the recruitment of the South African white diaspora. Andrucki points out that the South African agency responsible for recruiting the South African white diaspora associates 'white bodies' with skills, competence, development, economic growth and stability. The concept itself has been indirectly addressed by Fanon (1986) from a psychoanalytic perspective, looking particularly at how black bodies are perceived and treated by white bodies.

product you are selling is not original. That is why some Angolan businesses with a lot of capital prefer to hire Portuguese migrants and pay more because employing a white face results in lots of miracles happening. It is a market-ing strategy, this is how things work here – this applies not just to business here in Lubango. People have significant respect for a Portuguese migrant person. If you open a business and a Portuguese migrant opens the same business, I can tell you that people here will go and buy from the Portuguese migrant. Have you noticed that most of the supermarket workers here in Lubango have white faces? This is a marketing strategy (Tomas, Lubango, September 2015).

Tomas' statement might sound like self-hate but Fanon (1986) charac-terised this as a usual condition of postcolonial societies that equate white-ness with everything that is positive and blackness with everything that is negative. Tomas indirectly contrasts Portuguese migrants (white) and mi-grants from the DRC Congo (black) and represents one group as trustwor-thy and the other as untrustworthy. These dynamics also extend to private universities and schools, where the hiring of Portuguese lecturers and teachers is assumed to be a guarantee of the quality of education. Solange, who sends her children to a private school in Lubango, stated

I send my children to a private school because they have Portuguese teachers. Portuguese teachers are really good and they are not like Angolans. They do not take gasosa*. Children taught by Portuguese teachers learn well* (Solange, Lubango, October 2015).

The statements of Tomas and Solange, who are both black Angolans, ex-press and reveal another aspect of the deep and disturbing psychological impact of the coloniality of power in Lubango that associates Portuguese migrants with honesty and trust, and black-skinned Africans with the op-posite.

5.6 The trust in white bodies

Portuguese migrants – and white people in general – are endowed with ex-cessive trustworthiness in Lubango. This trust is linked to strong and es-sentialised cultural differences that are superficially contrasted between Portuguese migrants and Angolans and their respective attributes. As such, trustworthiness is one attribute that is assumed to be typical of Portuguese migrants' culture and can be compared with the differences in economic development between Angola and Portugal and the failures of Angola's acute social problems, which are attributed to culture differences. This is somewhat of a contradiction because, on the one hand, Portuguese migrants and Angolans claim that the Portuguese cultural influence, the language in particular, is one of the exceptions that makes them relatively more acceptable in comparison to other migrants like those from West Africa, the Congo or China. However, when it comes to trustworthiness and work ethics, the discourse tends to change and focuses instead on the cultural superiority of Portuguese migrants as a distinctive factor. This discourse, however, is used by both Portuguese migrants and Angolans. Critically looking at these dynamics, the trust accorded to Portuguese migrants is somehow linked to the deep inferiority complexes and Afro-pessimism which continue to dominate sectors of Lubango's society. When I asked Bety why she prefers to go to Sabina's beauty salon, which is more expensive, rather than going to a salon run by Angolans doing exactly the same job, she responded by saying:

> *You, who spent too much time outside of Angola, you do not understand how things work here in Lubango. People here trust the Portuguese migrants because they see them as serious and professional. These people are coming from Europe, they are accustomed to being professional. If they say they will call you then they call. If they say you can come for an appointment, then they have a place reserved for you. They are used to keeping their word because they have a different culture and standards of work. That is why I have my nails done at Sabina's beauty salon. She is always professional while the Angolan salons are always busy and you have to wait. They tell you to come even when they are fully booked* (Bety, Lubango, September 2015).

Bety's statement is based on strong stereotypes as well as on her personal experience as a client. In spite of Bety claiming that she trusts Portuguese migrants because of their professionalism, what seems to be at play here is class – and in particular her financial situation, which means that she can afford the services of Portuguese migrants, who tend to be more expensive and reserved for the select few. Those who can afford it feel superior, because there is a certain prestige attached to being able to afford services provided by Portuguese migrants in Lubango. Beneath the trust lies the psychological assumption that Sabine's salon is better than those of the Angolans because she comes from Europe and her services are expensive. Similar dynamics are observable in those Angolan businesses – such as Daniel's company (as mentioned in Chapter 4) – that hire Portuguese migrants. Whilst Angolans place excessive trust in Portuguese migrants, the reverse direction of trust cannot be said of Portuguese migrants, for they are reluctant to trust Angolans, particularly when it comes to work performance. Abel, a highly skilled Angolan, testifies that:

In the beginning it was very hard for my Portuguese colleagues to trust me. When I said that I had worked on this project before and I know what needs to be done, some of my Portuguese colleagues did not believe me. They did not expect to find someone like me here in Lubango. It took a while to win their trust. I felt like I needed to prove myself all the time. It used to bother me, but now I just do my work without worrying whether they trust me or not. But this is not the problem of the Portuguese migrants alone – Angolan colleagues are even worse. They do not trust each other at all. They feel like they always have to consult with a Portuguese colleague even for the small things. This attitude also extends to our government, which depends so much on Portuguese consultants and advisors. There are certain things in Angola that can be done by Angolans but they prefer to bring in Portuguese migrants. Go to some of these construction companies that work with the government and you will find a Portuguese migrant working as a truck driver there. This is a mentality problem. You have Portuguese people doing jobs that could be done by Angolans. Do you really think you need a truck driver from Portugal here? Nevertheless, they prefer to bring in Portuguese migrants because they trust the Portuguese. The same can be said of the Chinese – they do everything here. Even the plumbing in Lubango is done by the Chinese. Some say it is because the Chinese are hard-working but I do not know about that. I can only say that Angolans and the Angolan government do not trust Angolans and they expect everything to be done by foreigners, even things that can be done by Angolans (Abel, Lubango, September 2015).

Abel's analysis locates the problem of trust in Portuguese migrants not just at the level of the Angolan people but also at that of the Angolan government, which depends on this foreign workforce for everything. It is certainly legitimate for states, from time to time, to import migrant labour to fill a shortage on the labour market. However, what is interesting to observe in the case of Angola is that some of this imported labour does not have much to do with shortages on the labour market but, rather, with trust. In this regard, Alfredo states that

There was a time here in Angola in 2009 to 2013 when people had lots of money. In Luanda, some people used to import childminders from the Philippines. These are not the 'rich' rich but normal people with good salaries. They say that it's because they want their children to grow up speaking English but, in the Philippines, they do not have English as the official language.[55] *Then they say it is because Filipino nannies are trustworthy and do not steal and are faithful. This is the madness in Angola – everything that comes from outside is better. If it comes from Europe, it is like coming from paradise. Some of these rich Angolans have butlers from Portugal and they pay them lots of money. I do not know if you need that but money here is spent just to show off* (Alfredo, Lubango, September 2015).

This narrative would seem to indicate that the trust in Portuguese migrants is something that has dominated Lubango – and Angola in general. It does not seem to be linked to Portuguese migrants alone. Trust in this context has to do with the belief that Angolans do not have the capacity to carry out certain tasks. In other words, there is an indirect belief in the limitation of Angolans' ability to execute even what might be considered to be 'easy' tasks, like truck-driving for a construction company or looking after children. As a consequence, any criticism of these practices is reduced to the culture of the good work ethic, which is assumed to be a unique characteristic which Portuguese migrants and other foreigners have in comparison to Angolans.

5.7 The discourse of the Portuguese migrant work ethic

Portuguese migrants in Angola benefit from being trusted not only because they come from Europe and because, in Angola, there is certain admiration of all things European but also because of their supposed work ethic. The work ethic has long been debated in sociology and anthropology as a concept that certain ethnic groups, countries and cultures have adopted that helps them to succeed or fail (Fukayama 1996). The discourse of work ethics dismisses questions of economic structure and other complexities involved in social mobility and tends to focus on personal responsibility as a key pre-requisite for success. In the case of Portuguese migration to Angola, the notion of work ethics has been used as one of the unique characteristics of Portuguese migrants' social mobility and better working conditions. Interestingly, discourses on work ethics are deployed and internalised by both Portuguese migrants and Angolans. For Portuguese migrants, the work ethic functions as a shield to justify and protect privileges such as salaries and working conditions. In other words, An-

---

55 Filipinos with a good level of education do speak English and they are hired around the world as 'nannies'.

golans do not have what they want because they do not work hard enough. If they could, they would also enjoy social mobility. For those Portuguese migrants who made it, they attributed their success to their work ethic rather than to a combination of factors, as explained earlier. For some of my participants, Angola is considered a land of opportunity, the new *El Dorado* where those who work hard and have cultural capital like education and social capital in the form of local collaborators can succeed in life. This view is shared by a Portuguese businessman, Ernesto, when he says that:

> *There are lots of opportunities here in Angola. If you work hard you can make it here. I came here in 2003 with almost nothing but, today, my company offers services in most provinces of the southern part of Angola. You just need to have a vision and work hard. Most Portuguese that I know work really hard, that is why they can make it here. In Angola the key for success is work and nothing else. The conditions are perfect here. In Portugal, you have so many people competing for the same thing. Here in Angola there is not much competition and all you need is vision and hard work* (Ernesto, Lubango, August 2015).

The interesting thing about Ernesto's statement is that his company was not founded only on his good work ethic, as he had suggested – he is also in partnership with a white Angolan with strong links to the government. Links between the private sector and the government are common practice in Angola (Soares de Oliveira 2015). As such, most Portuguese companies operating in Angola are directly or indirectly linked to the Angolan government or to an oligarch with strong links with the MPLA (Åkesson 2018). The other interesting aspect of Ernesto's analysis is the neglect of other factors such as ethnic capital, which indirectly aids Portuguese migrants' social mobility. Although there are other factors at play in favour of Portuguese migrants, most of them insist that their social mobility and financial stability are due to their work ethic. This view, however, is also shared by a sector of Angolan society, especially those who think they have been successful economically, as Bety stated:

> *I do not want to say too much but there are many opportunities for people to succeed. This is not only for Portuguese migrants – look at other foreign groups like the* Mamadou *and the* langa*. They come here without money but after a year they can open a shop. The Chinese do the same. Why are the Angolans complaining if foreigners who come here are doing well in our country? You see, the problem with Angolans is that they do not like to work, that is the problem here. It is nothing to do with Portuguese migrants*

but rather it is about work. Angolans want to have a good life without work-
ing for it and they are always complaining about the government. The gov-
ernment cannot do everything. Angolans are lazy, the Chinese cannot speak
Portuguese well but they manage run their business here. The same can be
said about Mamadous *and* langas, *whereas Angolans want everything from*
the government, yet they want to get rich quickly. You need to work, the Por-
tuguese work hard. Look at Sabina, she came here and, after a while, she
now has her own salon (Bety, Lubango, September 2015).

Bety's position is common among Angolans who think that they have
made it socially and economically through their hard work. However,
Schubert (2017) points out that, in Angola, even a job guarantee is linked
to bribery and connections. Nevertheless, Bety's assessment is somehow
linked to what Schubert's (2017) participants called *cultural immediatism* –
i.e., the desire to get rich quickly in imitation of the extravagant lifestyle of
the elite. However, the discourse of the good work ethic, as demonstrated
by Bety and Ernesto, has become a message used by the Angolan government to dismiss any criticism of its failing service delivery and of its dependency on a foreign workforce as a result of Angolans' lack of personal responsibility and good work ethic (Schubert 2017). These dynamics of using the work ethic and personal responsibility are also evident in the work
of Armbruster (2010). According to her, German migrants in Namibia also
attribute their social and economic mobility to their strong work ethic and
personal responsibility rather than to structures and networks that allow
the privileged European to flourish in a context rife with social injustice
and inequality. The question here is not so much whether or not the work
ethic plays a role in the economic advancement of certain groups but more
that, in the case of both Angola and Namibia, there is a combination of
factors at play. Therefore, if Portuguese migrants' social mobility in Lubango is credited to their work ethic, the obvious implication is that Angolans
who do not make it economically are lazy, as suggested by Bety.

5.8 The discourse of the lazy native

If Portuguese migrants discursively represent themselves as having the typical Portuguese cultural trait of a strong work ethic which is connected to
their apparent social mobility in Angola, Angolans, on the other hand, are
represented as devoid of such a trait. By implication, Angolans are stereotypically presented as lazy and prone to partying, as Bety has suggested.
Ernesto and Bety had already hinted at how the discourse of the lazy native

operates when referring to the uniqueness of Portuguese migrants' positive work ethic. So, the discourse of the work ethic is contrasted with the normative discourse of the lazy native – which is rooted in Portuguese colonialism (see Chapter 4). The coloniality of power represents the lazy native as an Angolan who needs the constant supervision of Portuguese migrants. Angolans are seen as being able to do very little without foreign intervention, because Angolans can only work properly with strong surveillance, as hinted at by Daniel. Some of my Portuguese migrant and Angolan participants in this research routinely used the discourse of the lazy native to refer to issues concerning punctuality and the 'attitude' to work. If the discourse of the work ethic serves to justify and protect the privileges of Portuguese migrants, the lazy native has served to normalise the exclusion of Angolans through anecdotal experience and the stereotypical representation of the experience of working with Angolans. There are two aspects on which the lazy native stereotype is based: punctuality and attitude to work. First, punctuality has been one of the most lamented topics by Portuguese migrants, especially those in leadership positions. Stereotypically, Angolans are represented as having no concept of time, which is interpreted by some Portuguese migrants and Angolans as a problem of laziness and not taking work seriously. Justino, a Portuguese migrant manager, stated:

> *I have been working here in Lubango for the last three years but, before that, I worked in Luanda for two years. I can tell you that I have a very good relationship here with Angolans. However, working with Angolans is sometimes not so easy. They turn up late for work – not all, but most of them. We have here in the company what we call the Friday syndrome. Angolans do not come to work on Friday because the weekend starts then. Sometimes we also have the Monday syndrome; Angolans are hardly ever on time on a Monday. This is not to say that Angolans are bad, just that sometimes you have these problems with time and with them not taking work seriously. As a manager, I have to deal with all these syndromes. If people can arrive on time, then you can do more* (Justino, Lubango, October 2015).

Justino's observation does not take into consideration the fact that the company where he is manager is located outside the town, without proper public transport. What is more, the company only offers transportation for Portuguese migrants, while Angolan workers mostly have to depend on unreliable public transport. So it is not altogether surprising that Justino had a problem with time with his Angolan workers. As for the Friday and Monday syndromes, these might well be related to demotivation. Some workers shared privately with me that they are working without permanent contracts and are poorly and irregularly paid.[56] Such problems might have an effect on their supposed lack of a work ethic.

The second element which is related to the work ethic is a person's attitude to work. Bety thinks that:

> *Angolans like to party, they do not like to work. If you ask them to work, they will not do it but if you organise a party they will come. I am telling you, this is how things work here. The Portuguese know how to separate work and partying but the Angolans don't* (Bety, Lubango, September 2015).

A person's attitude to work is one element of the Eurocentric imagination, which allegedly 'explains' why certain groups prosper economically while others fail. Bety's generalisations are also shared by Etounga-Manguelle (2000) in his description of why Africans needs cultural adjustment, which includes the attitude to work or the work ethic. In the case of Portuguese migration to Angola, the attitude to work is used as a discourse by both Portuguese migrants and Angolans connected to the government in order to promote Portuguese migration and, at the same time, impede the social mobility of Angolans. Moreover, it is used as justification for their dependence on foreign workforces. The anomaly here is that, while countries in the global North depend on cheap labour to support certain sectors of their economy, in the case of Angola, there is a dependency on expensive foreign labour to maintain certain sectors of the economy. The irony is that the Angolan labour market depends on foreign labour regardless of the need, justifying this with the colonialist argument of the Angolans' poor attitude to work.

5.9 The issue of Portuguese migrants as agents of development

Portuguese migrants use the 'work ethic' and the 'lazy native' as discourses to justify their own presence, blaming the lack of skilled Angolans on the

---

56 At the time that this research was conducted, Angola was going through an economic crisis as oil prices plunged. Some Portuguese migrants also complained that their salaries were no longer paid on time and that they also had tremendous difficulty in sending remittances to Portugal because the banks had placed restrictions on the amount of money that they could send. The situation led to frustration and despair and, by 2016, some participants had moved back to Portugal while others preferred to stay in Angola, hoping for an improvement in the economic situation there.

long years of civil war, thereby characterising Portuguese migration to Angola as a humanitarian gesture. Some Portuguese migrants do not see themselves as labour migrants but as development or humanitarian agents who are on a mission to support and modernise Angola. This can be seen in the emphasis put by my Portuguese participants on the role of the entrepreneurial success of the Portuguese private company in work, rather than on the complex partnerships between these companies and the Angolan government. This is because, on the one hand, the Portuguese migration trajectory is linked to the economic crisis of 2008 and because, on the other, there is the social reality of the unconventional place in which they are working. As such, the tendency of some Portuguese migrants is to imagine and equate their presence in Angola with that of development assistance – done by constantly emphasising the social problems in Angola as well as their desire to help. The issue here is not so much about the honesty of such a desire but about how the coloniality of power always imagines Africa as a place in difficulty, which needs to be helped and reshaped in the European image (Power 2003). Fernando, for example, does not connect his migration trajectory to the economic crisis at all; rather, he sees it as a contribution to Angola. According to him:

> *I am not a migrant. I came here to help and to contribute to the development of the country. I had a job before I came here and I was not desperate to find work; the thing is that my skills are needed here, there is so much need here – people like me can contribute and help this country. I would like to settle here, buy a house and raise a family – and help; there is so much need here* (Fernando, Lubango, October 2015).

The case of Fernando is not unique. Other Portuguese migrants' relationship with Lubango always ends up with them speaking of their desire to help. According to Joana:

> *My objective in coming here was also to help the little children in Africa. I always wanted to do that in Africa. Some years ago, I wanted to volunteer to work on a project in Kenya because I am a nurse by profession, but the Kenya thing never really worked out. Today I am here where there is so much need. I have not done much with children yet because I am very busy with my lecturing job but I would like to one day work with African children, because I love African children and I want to help them* (Joana, Lubango, October 2015).

Both Fernando and Joana speak of their particular longing to provide assistance to Angola. In other words, in spite of both being paid for their work in Angola, their relationship to the country continues to be based on Angola's needs. They cannot see themselves as migrants – they must include the development aspect in their discourse because, subconsciously, that is what is expected of Europeans when they go to Africa.

5.10 Conclusion

Portuguese migration to Angola – and especially to Lubango – has been dominated by a number of factors. This chapter has demonstrated how the coloniality of power operates in Lubango through various discursive practices that are designed to enhance the symbolic power of Portuguese migrants in Angola. These discourses and practices focus on ethnic capital, uneven geographies of development and power, and cultural aspects – all of which are used as justification for the Portuguese privilege in Angola. The justification includes aspects such as the Portuguese work ethic and attitude to work and the lazy native. Moreover, Portuguese migrants' privileges in Lubango also include better salaries and work conditions. The Portuguese symbolic power which operates through the coloniality of power has been challenged in Lubango by two groups, both directly and indirectly. The first group is the Angolan migration officials who used the lax Angolan visa regime as a way to limit the symbolic power which Portuguese migrants have in their place of work. The Angolan visa regime has been one of the most difficult obstacles challenging and limiting Portuguese migrants' symbolic power. The Portuguese are admired but face significant challenges when it comes to obtaining visas. The limitation of Portuguese symbolic power by Angolan migration officials has been interpreted by Portuguese migrants as a consequence of anti-Portuguese sentiments. However, further analysis indicates that such actions are common state practice and that Angolans also face hurdles in obtaining visas to Portugal. Moreover, most Portuguese migrants are not necessarily used to having their EU member-state citizenship privileges challenged, in particular in a postcolonial context like Lubango. Therefore, it is common to equate the Angolan bureaucratic visa regime to anti-Portuguese sentiments. This is not, however, to say that such sentiments do not exist but that it can better be understood by looking at visa problems from different perspectives.

Second, Angolans who were once migrants tend to see Portuguese symbolic power as an injustice and, in some cases, as undeserved. They see it as based not just on the skills that Portuguese migrants bring but on other factors, too. However, Angolans who were once migrants are discursively challenged by other Angolans and the Angolan state both of whom insist on promoting the notion that Portuguese social mobility in Angola is based on work ethics rather than other factors like race.

Chapter 6: Conclusion

The main and overriding research question of this thesis has been: 'How can Portuguese migration to Angola be explained?' Accordingly, I have argued that Portuguese migration to Angola should be understood not only within the framework of economic migration as a result of the economic crisis or as a skills-driven migration but also as a complex web of intersecting phenomena and processes. These latter elements include the Portuguese colonial legacy, family networks, discourses, myths, trust, the work ethic, Eurocentrism, 'race', Lusotropicalism, postcolonial state formation and the coloniality of power. These concepts, processes and phenomena and their attendant bodies of literature have been the multifaceted and cross-disciplinary theoretical scaffold surrounding my analysis throughout the foregoing chapters. In the first part of this concluding chapter, I summarise the contents and key findings of each chapter. This is followed by a synthesis of general findings. I then ask: 'What can we learn from the phenomenon of recent Portuguese migration to Angola?' In the final three short sections of the chapter I briefly assess the contribution of the thesis to the discipline of Human Geography and to the interdisciplinary field of Migration Studies, make some suggestions for future research which could build on what I present in my thesis and append some comments on policy.

6.1 Chapter highlights

The first chapter presented the core research problem, the study's aims and research questions, the rationale behind the study and its overall significance. The chapter also highlighted the demographic representation of Portuguese migrants in Angola and showed how this study can be situated within the wider disciplines of Migration Studies and Human Geography and attendant ongoing debates on interdisciplinarity.

The second chapter dealt with a review of the relevant research and critically pointed to the gap that exists in the migration literature, which is Eurocentric in its orientation, as it mainly focuses on the dominant South-North migration axis. The chapter argued that the hegemonic paradigm that privileges the importance of this South-North migration does not do justice to the complexities and ambiguities of other global migration dynamics. Such an approach from Europe and the global North is preoccupied with push and pull factors and emphasises the economic drivers that push migrants from the less-developed countries of the global South – considered as poor, unstable and with serious social inequalities – and pulls them towards the countries of the global North, considered as rich, politically and economically stable, with a strong middle class and an allegedly strong social formation. My critique of this approach was that it might not be helpful in understanding other dynamics such as South-South and North-South migration flows. The question here was not so much about the veracity of the South-North paradigm but its over-concentration at the expense of other migration dynamics and the subconscious assumption that migration from the global North to the global South is a relic of the colonial past. These assumptions are based on the economic and political gap between South and North – assumed to be an impediment that limits the occurrence of North-South migration. However, this latter assumption does not take into consideration the crisis that the current global capitalist system poses for migration, which constantly encourages new routes, the nature of which is not yet fully grasped by migration theories. Thus, the chapter demonstrated the conceptual limitations of and the gap existing in the literature on the hegemonic South-North and other dominant migration paradigms.

Chapter 3 set out the methods used to collect the research data for this study and justified their importance in addressing the key research questions on Portuguese migration to Lubango, Angola. The chapter also dealt with the challenges involved in researching migration in the context of Lubango and Lisbon, dominated as it is by power dynamics of race and class. I also set out issues regarding the researcher's positionality and engaged in some reflexive considerations about doing fieldwork with Portuguese migrants in Angola.

Chapter 4 is the first of the two main empirical chapters, although both are strongly encased within my theoretical scaffold. Particular emphasis in Chapter 4 was given to the roots of Lusotropicalism and its subsequent legacy in Portugal and Angola. The chapter concentrated on three distict elements: (i) the roots of Lusotropicalism in Brazil, (ii) the Lusotropicalist legacy in Portugal and postcolonial Angola and (iii) the myth of Lusotropicalism in dealing with race relations in postcolonial Angola. Lusotropicalism was seen as having had a significant impact both on the representation of Portuguese colonialism as benevolent and on race relations as amicable – with no signs of apartheid – in comparison with other colonial powers, especially those operating elsewhere in Africa. My account demonstrated that racism was practised in the Portuguese colonies of Brazil and Angola without being the result of a system like apartheid. Because of the supposed benevolent Portuguese colonial system, Lusotropicalism had significantly impacted on the way in which the Portuguese saw themselves in relation both to their colonial history and to the question of black migrants in Portugal. Lusotropicalism did not directly influence Portugal but it did dominate postcolonial Angolan race relations – in particular its nation-state formation – which tended to emphasise and impose the myth of common descent instead of diversity, as is the case in South Africa. Lusotropicalism in postcolonial Angola included the adoption and appreciation of the Portuguese language and cultural etiquette as signs of civilisation; often these were enmeshed in family lineages and networks. Much of this legacy is associated with the country's postcolonial national formation, which was dominated by former assimilates and 'civilised' black, white and mixed-race Angolans who tried to construct a national identity based on a distorted urban myth and a civilised and assimilated Angolan and socialist modernism. As a result, although racism and class were ignored, at least officially, they were subtly applied in certain professions and trades in the private sector of Lubango. Here, whiteness continued to be admired and associated with superiority and material and psychological wellbeing.

Chapter 5, the second core analytical chapter, examined the coloniality of power and explored how being Portuguese and coming from Portugal are factors that contribute to an uncritical acceptance of Portuguese migrants in Angola. Thus, it looked at the role of uneven geographies of power between Angola and Portugal and at how these power asymmetries helped Portuguese migrants to secure jobs as well as good salaries. This often happens under the myth of expatriates' skills and work ethic, set against the myth of the 'lazy native'. Particular attention in this chapter was devoted to the plastic concept of skill and to the way that higher skill is an ambiguous variable in Angola, intersecting with race, class, geographical origin and the perceived value of foreign education. Several injustices were recorded, particularly amongst Angolan skilled workers who were paid and valued less than their Portuguese counterparts. Overall, the chapter clearly demonstrated that, in Lubango, the coloniality of power equates with whiteness and with Portugal – as developed and advanced, with positive cultural traits. On the other hand, some elements, which could arguably be regarded as 'revenge', were also documented, related to claims of anti-Portuguese discrimination exercised by the Angolan visa authorities and police.

6.2 General findings

This thesis has sought to problematise Portuguese migration to Angola as an element of the 'new' trend of migration dynamics from the global North to the global South. It has discussed the semi-peripheral or peripheral status of Portugal within Europe and explained the country's colonial history and legacy, as well as the combined concepts of uneven power geographies and of whiteness as providers of privilege for Portuguese migrants. My argument has been not so much about the positionality of Portugal within the world system but about the uneven and shifting relationship between Portugal and Angola. This historically fluctuating relationship was interpreted as being dependent on colonial and postcolonial statuses, on notions of core, periphery and semi-periphery and on Massey's (2005) 'power geometry'. Portuguese migrants are coming from a particular space that is imagined by local Angolans to be powerful, advanced and civilised; as such they are already moving into these advantageous and powerful positions, regardless of the skills they actually have. Åkesson and Orjuela (2019) have pointed out how Portuguese migrants view themselves as more 'developed' and more 'civilised' than Angolan natives. My thesis has confirmed that such a perception is not limited to the migrant sectors of Angolan society – in particular, those who think that they have made it economically also subscribe to the notion that Portuguese migrants are 'developed' and 'civilised' and come from a 'superior' continent.

In order to understand and explain Portuguese migration to Angola, the thesis has interwoven various theoretical, disciplinary and interdisciplinary frameworks. Prominent among them is postcolonial theory – in particular, the intersection of the past and the present – and how some aspects of the past continue to be part of the present in Lubango and the rest of Angola, even several decades after the end of Portuguese colonialism. In other words, I tend to see a symbolic continuation of the Portuguese presence in Lubango – a city that is enduringly stratified by race and class. With its long history of racial stratification, Lubango represents, in essence, a continuation of a Portuguese symbolic presence, as previous colonial boundaries of class and race continue, imaginatively and practically, to be part of the city. In this case, Portuguese migrants are moving to a space that is both imaginatively close and familiar but also geographically distant. The imaginative closeness is associated with the use of the Portuguese language and an admiration for the supposed Portuguese work culture. Here, it is important to observe the role played by former black assimilates and white and mixed-race Angolans in the formation of this closeness to Portugal.

The postcolonial Angolan state indirectly continues to encourage certain customs of Portuguese colonialism. Portuguese became the only officially recognised language, while African languages were dismissed as a source of tribalism and a sign of obscurantism and backwardness. Thus, there was a strong disregard for a multicultural, multi-ethnic society and the emphasis was put on common descent, as illustrated in Angola's popular culture and national anthem. To be Angolan came to be subtly associated with speaking Portuguese and having a Portuguese name – in a nutshell, to be Angolan has come to be associated with being 'civilised', 'assimilated' and as 'Portuguese' as possible. However, the state's postcolonial formation strategy had a different result. On the one hand, mastery of the Portuguese language and having a Portuguese name were used as means to identify who could be considered truly Angolan. On the other hand, not having a proper command of the Portuguese language or a Portuguese name were viewed in urban places like Luanda with suspicion, in particular if the names or Portuguese accent were associated with spaces controlled by the opposition factions, the FNLA and UNITA. This postcolonial position could be traced to Portuguese colonialism and, in particular, to the dichotomy between 'civilised' and 'uncivilised' and the geographical binary between the urban and the rural. This is no surprise for the many Angolan politicians who subscribe to these ideas, as they have been pejoratively called *creolos* by their critics (Soares de Oliveira 2015). The *creolos* continued to imaginatively define Portugal as 'the motherland, a developed place where the children of the elite can go to obtain an education, a place where the Angolan elite can go on holiday, conduct their international business and keep their fortune – obscurely obtained from natural resources' (Costa *et al.* 2014). In other words, Portugal continues to be a point of reference for the Angolan elite and a place for transnational activities for white and mixed-race Angolans, just as it was a place of destination for asylum-seekers during the civil war. The interesting thing about Angolans who sought asylum in Portugal during the civil war was the question of race; in order to deal with the issue – in particular the visibility of black migrants in Portugal – the old myth of Lusotropicalism again became the focal point. Racism was interpreted as an economic problem that could be solved with better schools, better housing and better integration, rather than seeing it as a structurally embedded social, psychological and behavioural problem. The myth of Lusotropicalism continues to indirectly play a role in understanding race relations in Portugal – in particular, the myth of the benevolent Portuguese colonial system and racial colour-blindness (Castelo 1998).

However, the notion of Lusotropicalism influenced not only Portugal's race relations but also Angola's postcolonial race relations, which were strongly shaped by the myth of Lusotropicalism, as this thesis has demonstrated. Racial stratification and hierarchies continue to be practised, albeit subtly, in postcolonial Angola and, in some cases, race continues to play a role in class formation and especially in employment – as I have shown in Lubango. This shows that whiteness continues to be admired and associated with prestige and superiority in postcolonial Angola. My thesis has thus demonstrated that Portuguese migrants in Lubango are moving to spaces where the coloniality of power is strongly active and where whiteness and Portugal are admired and associated with positive traits. One of the key ways to understand and explain the coloniality of power in Lubango is the idea that white Europeans are endowed with particular cultural traits that facilitate their entering the middle and higher echelons of the Angolan job market regardless of their skills. There is an unconsciously established belief among the locals that Portuguese migrants are superior and deserve better employment positions and better salaries. To this end, the thesis has demonstrated how the so-called superiority of Portuguese migrants is justified through the construct of a discourse of work ethics and trust. These cultural traits are essentialised and considered as typical of Portuguese migrants and are reasons justifying why they deserve better salaries and special treatment, in comparison to other migrants from the DRC (Congo), West Africa and China. Migrants from other countries are considered as different 'others' and Angolans often used derogatory terms when talking about them while, in the case of Portuguese migrants, Angolans sympathetically call them *povo irmão* (our brothers from Portugal). In spite of this admiration for Portuguese migrants, I have pointed out that there are latent conflicts between Angolans and Portuguese which are linked to the nature of Angola's visa bureaucracy and to a jealousy rooted mostly in the difference in working conditions and salaries. However, these conflicts are not strong enough to amount to anti-Portuguese political mobilisation. The general tendency is to see Portuguese migration in a positive light because it is discursively associated with Angolan development, regardless of whether or not this is really the case. In the light of the above arguments, a few broader lessons can be learnt from this type of migration.

6.3 What can we learn from Portuguese migration to Angola?

The first thing that can be learnt from Portuguese migration to Angola is that it is complex, ambiguous and unpredictable. Whilst it is framed by economic factors, such as the growth of the Angolan economy and the years of the financial crisis in Portugal, it is also strongly linked to the nature and history of Portuguese colonialism. It is almost impossible to understand some of the dynamics involved in Portuguese migration to Angola without tracing them back to the Portuguese colonial legacy. Therefore, this study has sought to selectively engage with aspects of Portuguese colonialism that continue to play a role in Angolan society to this day and which facilitate Portuguese migration to Angola – for example by helping Portuguese migrants to enter the Angolan job market. This selective colonial legacy includes family networks, language and Portuguese migrants' positive cultural traits. Most of these selective legacies were expressed by my participants in the form of a common narrative linking this migration trajectory not only to the global economic crisis but also to the Portuguese colonial legacy.

Second, the functional concept of semi-periphery (Arrighi 1985) is theoretically significant in understanding Portuguese migration dynamics as including both receiving and sending countries but it also needs to be linked to the legacy of colonial power. In other words, although Portuguese migrants might come from the periphery of Europe and from the global semi-periphery, they have significant power and privilege in Angola which is more or less equal to that enjoyed by the migrants of developed countries globally. This power and privilege is rooted not only in the colonial legacy of Europe but also in the notion of uneven geographies – described by Massey (2005) as 'power geometry'. According to Massey, citizens moving from supposedly developed to underdeveloped countries have symbolic power. Portuguese migrants going to Angola possess advantages and ethnic capital in a context where coming from Portugal and being white is admired. This research has demonstrated empirically how the geographies (or geometries) of power rooted in various factors can help Portuguese migrants to have symbolic power in Lubango.

Third, Portuguese migrants are moving to spaces that have already been historically racialised, where white and mixed-race Angolans already hold economic, political and symbolic power and where black Angolans unconsciously know where their place in society is. It is not an overstatement to argue that the racial hierarchies left by Portuguese colonialism still play a significant role in Lubango. Thus, my thesis has not in any way argued that racial stratification in Lubango is the result of the presence of Portuguese migrants but that such stratification is the result of a long historical process of racialisation there. The division of labour associates whiteness with management or leadership. Whiteness is admired and respected whereas blackness continues to be associated with old colonial stereotypes of the 'lazy native' and of black workers' limited capacity. These negative stereotypes are subtly used as a discursive justification to exclude black Angolans from employment in certain sectors – in particular, well-paid jobs in the private sector. Black Angolans are discursively constructed and represented as prone to easy gratification and not taking work seriously; hence their exclusion from positions of responsibility. Therefore, my thesis has shown that, in order to understand Portuguese migration to Lubango, it is important to also include the longer-established role of white and mixed-race Angolans.

Fourth, this thesis has revealed that the dynamics of Portuguese migration to Lubango are also observable and applicable in other colonised spaces, where former colonists still have symbolic power and privileges. Armbruster's (2010) study of German migrants in Namibia and Andrucki's (2017) on white migrants in South Africa both indicate similar patterns, whereby migrants from the global North enjoy certain privileges in sub-Saharan Africa. As such it is possible to generalise the findings from this thesis – that postcolonial encounters are still based on the different power relations between the dominant and the subordinate. In particular, migration from one global space to another is viewed differently, as South-North movement is largely seen in a negative light while North-South flows are viewed positively. Furthermore, Hayes and Pérez Gañán's (2017) study on Spanish migrants in Ecuador after the global financial crisis of 2008 reinforces some of my findings. Spanish migrants in Ecuador also enjoy certain privileges – what Hayes (2014) called 'geographic arbitrage' – whereby individuals with a positive economic and symbolic status move across borders to take advantage of better opportunities in a particular transnational social field, corresponding to a postcolonial, globalised division of labour.

Finally, my thesis has shown that Portuguese migration to Angola brings into focus the coloniality of power, a concept that was developed in South America by Maldonado-Torres (2010) but is applicable in the African context. Thus the thesis has combined the coloniality of power and Massey's (2005) concepts of power geometry and uneven global geographies to empirically look at how European ethnic capital operates. What is more, it demonstrates that, in the case of Lubango, the coloniality of power also lies in the nature of Portuguese colonialism and postcolonialism. In other words, part of the effect of coloniality is the inherited structural advantage of those migrating from the ex-colonial metropole to within the Lusophone migratory space; these migrants carry the 'ethnic capital' of 'whiteness' and former colonial domination to a country where such privilege still pays. 'Skilled white bodies' (Andrucki 2017; Augusto and King 2020) command a wage and salary premium on the Angolan labour market, both for themselves and for the Angolan businesses that employ them. However, during my fieldwork, I discovered that 'skill' is a plastic concept in Angola and that many supposedly skilled Portuguese migrants there were doing relatively unskilled jobs. Nevertheless, many Portuguese were promoted beyond their actual skill and qualification levels, to the justified annoyance of local skilled personnel.

6.4 Contribution to the disciplines of Migration Studies and Geography

As mentioned earlier in the thesis, Portuguese migration to Lubango represents an opportunity for a new interdisciplinary migration theory to be explored in order to explain this seemly unique North-South migration trajectory. The thesis has recognised the crudeness of the North-South global geographical binary and has sought to explore the dynamics of Portuguese migration to Lubango in light of the functional concept of semi-periphery (Arrighi 1985). The geographical notion of 'Portugal as periphery' or, in a more nuanced analysis, as 'semi-periphery', draws on a tradition of geographical, economic, international relations and development studies literature centred around the overarching dualistic concept of core–periphery applied to Portugal (Holland 1979), Southern Europe (Arrighi 1985), Europe as a whole (Seers 1979) and the world (Wallerstein 1976). As King (2019) has recently argued, global economic developments of the past two or three decades have re-positioned Portugal again in the 'South' of the global North, whilst oil-spurred development in Angola has arguably temporarily elevated the country to the 'North' of the global South. One can suggest, therefore, that Portugal holds a special place within the European and global map of international migration, exemplifying the conditions of both core (of the Lusophone migration system) and periphery (to the European migration system) at the same time, thereby justifying the label of semi-periphery. However, as Åkesson and Orjuela (2019: 231) point out, the influx of Portuguese migrants to Angola has resulted in ambiguous and contradictory relations of dependency, whereby the migrants' image of themselves (also in the eyes of many Angolans) as more 'developed' and 'civilised' than the 'natives' clashes with their new position of subordination to the corrupt and unpredictable mechanisms of the Angolan state. These dynamics, as pointed out, tend to be complex; in some cases, Portuguese migrants face bureaucratic visa challenges but, in others, they are also treated as superior.

In discussing the complexity of Portuguese migration to Angola, this thesis has provided empirical insights into the ongoing debate about North-South migration within the field of Human Geography. It has done this by exploring the dynamics of intersectionality, history, race and uneven geographies which are key components to understand Portuguese migration to Angola. Portuguese migration to Angola is welcomed and partly accepted because of the imaginative geographies that Angolans have about Europe and Portugal in particular. Portuguese migrants are moving from supposedly 'superior' spaces into 'inferior' spaces that permit them to have certain advantages, privileges and power. The thesis thus empirically corroborates Massey's (2005) notion of power geometry and the idea that migration and mobility are dominated not only by economics or capital but also by race, gender and class; all of these set within the shifting terrain of global geopolitics and uneven development. Generally, migrants moving from countries that are considered developed have significant power when they move to countries considered less developed. Thus, Portuguese migrants are more welcome than other migrants, this preferential treatment reflecting both the Portuguese colonial legacy and Portugal's status as a 'white' European country. In other words, there is a combination of race and geography. In Lubango, being white and coming from Portugal is still somehow admired and associated with positive cultural traits. My field site has thus proven to be an ideal spatial laboratory in which to observe the interplay of migration, race, ethnic capital, migrant–host relations and the geographies of employment in a segmented and colonially shaped labour market. Here, these processes and interactions, typical of many of the new (and old) dynamics of North-South migration, unfold in a microcosm.

Let me turn now to the question posed in the chapter subheading: 'How does my thesis relate to the fields of Geography and Migration Studies?' In Chapter 1, I argued that these two areas of study combine strongly together: Migration Studies as an interdisciplinary or postdisciplinary field (following Favell 2008), and Geography as arguably the broadest and most flexible academic discipline within which to study migration in its multiple and always spatially embedded forms (after King 2012). The research that I have carried out and presented in this thesis exemplifies this proficuous combination of approaches. Throughout my conceptual and empirical chapters I have drawn from ideas and frameworks from several disciplines – economics, history, sociology, anthropology and, of course, human and regional geography – and blended them together in what I believe is a truly interdisciplinary or, indeed, postdisciplinary analysis. Yet, I have privileged – and drawn particular inspiration from – writers who are geographers and/or who have espoused geographical concepts in studying migration. Terms such as power geometries, geographies of uneven development and hierarchies of core, periphery and semi-periphery are obvious examples which have resonated through my account.

The power of the discipline of geography to critically inform research on migration is aptly summarised by Hardwick (2008), who identifies three main theoretical strands: (i) the neopositivist approach of population geographers and their contributions to socio-spatial theory in explaining migration patterns and flows; (ii) the many contributions of human geographers to the study of transnationalism, including family, social and ethnic networks; and (iii) critical race theory and whiteness studies.

Without going into too much repetitive detail, I would claim that this thesis has advanced these three agendas and others, too. Firstly, I have attempted to 'explain' Portuguese migration to Angola both in terms of economic forces and in relation to the history of colonialism. Both are necessary to account for this particular North-to-South migration, which is uncommon in a migration world dominated by South-North flows. On the economic front, I referred to the post-2008 economic crisis in Portugal, the booming oil and construction economy of Angola and the unequal geography of cores and peripheries rooted in colonialism. The history of colonial relations was excavated to expose the pernicious survival of colonial-era social, racial and attitudinal structures into the post-independence period. I deployed the concepts of Lusotropicalism and coloniality to interpret how the 'objective facts' of this North-South migration, one of the few examples of the migration of 'northerners' to sub-Saharan Africa, played out in the complex reality of contemporary Angolan society.

Secondly, I investigated the transnational family and social networks which underpinned part of the Portugal-to-Angola migratory phenomenon; these networks, too, were embedded in the history of Portuguese colonial settlement in Angola, including the post-independence repatriation of the *retornados* in the mid-1970s. This enabled some Portuguese migrants, who have arrived in Angola in the last decade or so, to draw on prior ancestral linkages to colonial-era migrations, to build on cross-generational family and social networks and to develop what I called 'ethnic capital'.

Finally, I have emphasised the relevance of 'race' and 'culture' in this migration, framed by colonial power relations between the capital of a former colonial empire and a sub-Saharan African ex-colony. Throughout the thesis I have made explicit the 'racial' element of Portuguese migration to Angola and how it fits in with the complex racial and class politics of postcolonial Angolan society. Within Angola, the socio-ethnic divisions between white, mixed-race and black Angolans were also drawn out, as well as the rural–urban dichotomy within Angolan society. The notion of Portuguese migrants as privileged 'skilled white bodies' (Augusto and King 2020) was crucial to this analysis, developed particularly in Chapter 5.

6.5 Suggestions for further research

The research findings and associated discussions in this thesis lead me to suggest five issues concerning Portuguese migration to Angola that could be explored further. The first of these is gender; although a small majority of my participants were female, the question of gender was not fully explored. Further research could include questions such as:

– What does it mean to be a female Portuguese migrant working in Angola?
– What are some of the obstacles that Portuguese female migrants face?
– How does the gendered experience of migration (of both male and female migrants) intersect with issues of race and racialised sexuality?
– Are there any associations that deal with issues related to Portuguese female migrants?

Although Portuguese migration to Angola, like most migrations of highly skilled and expat people from the global North to the global South, is thought to be predominantly male, there are clearly many Portuguese female migrants – some working independently in Angola, some working at universities as teachers and administrators, some in shops and supermarkets as cashiers and others who are there with their Portuguese partners – and there are also Portuguese migrants married to Angolans.

Secondly, the thesis has not directly dealt with the question of transnationalism. Given the nature and complexity of the Portuguese colonial legacy, there are many transnational activities taking place between Angola and Portugal, more notably by those who hold dual citizenship and who live between Portugal and Lubango. The topic of ongoing transnational activities could also be explored for further research.

Third, there is intense cooperation between Portuguese and Angolan companies in certain sectors of Portuguese society; when speaking of Portuguese migration to Angola, the emphasis seems always to concentrate on Portuguese companies working in Angola, as if most of this migration depends on them. My study did not directly address this question. There is a strong relationship in some cases between Portuguese migration to Angola and Portuguese construction companies but that is only one part of this migration system.

Fourthly, the study did not make a direct comparison between Portuguese migration to Angola and Angolan migration to Portugal – although it would be interesting to do a comparative study. The analytical lens of 'skill' could be an interesting vehicle for such a comparison, I suggest. The way in which Portuguese migrants in Angola are able to enhance the value of their skills endowment and to be considered highly skilled, even when they are not, could be contrasted with the inverse effect suffered by Angolan migrants in Portugal, whose skills are downplayed and devalued because of the way they are regarded as only fit for unskilled jobs in the Portuguese labour market. Additionally, it would also be interesting to conduct research comparing the different migrants groups such as the Chinese, West Africans, those from the DRC and Portuguese migrants.

Finally, a comparison of visa regimes between Portugal and Angola would also be an interesting research topic; it seems that both countries have a love–hate relationship when it comes to dealing with visa requirements. Most Portuguese migrants I spoke to during my fieldwork complained about the visa requirement as one of the factors that make their migration trajectory very difficult, at times forcing many to work illegally.

6.6 Policy contribution

The discourse of Portuguese migration to Angola revolves around the vague and plastic concept of skilled migration. However, there is no clear definition of a skilled Portuguese migrant. The discourse almost certainly gives the impression that to be white and Portuguese is equal to being skilled. This study has not attempted to negate the existence of skilled Portuguese migrants but has, instead, pointed out that not all Portuguese migration to Angola is dominated by skilled workers and not every Portuguese migration is linked to Portuguese companies. In cases where there is, indeed, a shortage of skills on the Angolan labour market, it would be best to create a platform where the local transfer of skills and knowledge can take place. However, most of the institutions that I visited had social hierarchies that seemed to prevent the exchange of knowledge from happening. For example, at one private university, Portuguese lecturers and Angolan lecturers rarely meet because the offices are divided according to nationality. They should create a platform where Portuguese migrants are not only working together in the same institution as Angolans but are collaborating in the transfer of knowledge and skills. Secondly, visa requirements in both Angola and Portugal are unnecessarily rigid. It would be best for both countries to work out a programme that would allow more flexibility for visa applications. For example, seasonal visa schemes could be one possible solution. Third, the Angolan government should be more open to embracing the diversity and multiculturalism that exists in Angola rather than continuing to indirectly encourage the myth of common descent. True, the Portuguese language and aspects of Portuguese culture have become part of Angola – a fact that remains irreversible – but to indirectly exclude African languages and discourage the use of African names as a sign of obscurantism would continue to exclude significant numbers of the population who still value their traditions. Thus, the Angolan government is indirectly continuing to perpetuate the old colonial divisions of civilised versus uncivilised and urban versus rural, which continue to play an exaggerated role in postcolonial Angola.

References

Abrahamsen, R. (2003) African studies and the postcolonial challenge. *African Affairs*, 102(407): 189–210.

Åkesson, L. (2016) Moving beyond the colonial era? New Portuguese migrants in Angola. *Cahiers d'Études Africaines*, 56(221–222): 267–285.

Åkesson, L. (2018) *Postcolonial Portuguese Migration to Angola*. Cham: Palgrave Macmillan.

Åkesson, L. and Orjuela, C. (2019) North-south migration and the corrupt other: practices of bribery among Portuguese migrants in Angola. *Geopolitics*, 24(1): 230–250.

Alatas, S. (1977) *The Myth of the Lazy Native*. London: Frank Cass.

Almeida, J. and Corkill, D. (2015) On being Portuguese: Lusotropicalism, migration and the politics of citizenship. In Rodriguez, E. and Tate, S. (eds) *Creolizing Europe: Legacies and Transformations*, pp. 157–174. Liverpool: Liverpool University Press.

Andrucki, M.J. (2017) 'Wish you were here': bodies, diaspora strategy and the politics of propinquity in post-apartheid. *Geographical Journal*, 183(1): 47–57.

Armbruster, H. (2010) Realising the self and developing the African: German immigrants in Namibia. *Journal of Ethnic and Migration Studies*, 36(8): 1229–1246.

Arrighi, G. (1985) *Semiperipheral Development: The Politics of Southern Europe in the Twentieth Century*. London: Sage.

Atkinson, A. (2015) *Inequality: What Can Be Done?* Princeton NJ: Harvard University Press.

Augusto, A. (2012) The Impact of the Angolan Political History on the Social Divisions among the Angolan Community in Bavaria – A Case Study. Berlin: Alice Salomon Hochschule, unpublished MA dissertation.

Augusto, A. and King, R. (2020) 'Skilled white bodies': Portuguese workers in Angola as a case of North-South migration. *Geographical Journal*, 186(1): 116–127.

Baganha, M.I. (2009) The Lusophone migratory system: patterns and trends. *International Migration*, 47(3): 5–20.

Bakewell, O. (2009) *South-South Migration and Human Development: Reflections on African Experiences*. New York: United Nations Development Program, online at http://hdr.undp.org/sites/default/files/hdrp_2009_07.pdf.

Bauder, H. (2006) *Labor Movement: How Migration Regulates Labor Markets*. Oxford: Oxford University Press.

Bauman, Z. (2004) *Wasted Lives: Modernity and its Outcasts*. Cambridge: Polity Press.

Beauchemin, C. (2018) Migration between Africa and Europe (MAFE): advantages and limitations of multi-site design. In Beauchemin, C. (ed.) *Migration between Africa and Europe*, pp. 11–33. Cham: Springer.

Bender, G. (2004) *Angola under the Portuguese: Myth and Reality*. Trenton NJ: Africa World Press.

Berg, B. (2004) *Qualitative Research Methods*. Boston: Pearson.

Betts, A. and Collier, P. (2017) *Refugees Transforming a Broken System*. Milton Keynes: Penguin/Random House.

Bhabha, H. (1994) *The Location of Culture*. New York: Routledge.

Bhabha, H. and Comaroff, J. (2002) Speaking of postcoloniality in the continuous present: a conversation. In Goldberg, D. and Quayson, A. (eds) *Relocating Post-colonialism*, pp. 15–46. Oxford: Blackwell.

Bhambra, G.K. (2014) *Connected Sociologies: Theory for a Global Age*. London: Bloomsbury.

Bhopal, K. (2018). *White Privilege: The Myth of a Post-Racial Society*. Bristol: Policy Press.

Birmingham, D. (2006) *Empire in Africa: Angola and its Neighbors*. Athens OH: Ohio University Press.

Bodemann, M. and Yurdakul, G. eds (2006) *Migration, Citizenship, Ethnos*. New York: Palgrave Macmillan.

Bonilla-Silva, E. (2006) *Racism Without Racists*. Oxford: Rowman & Littlefield.

Bourdieu, P. (1982) The forms of capital. In Richardson, J.G. (ed.) *Handbook of Theory and Research for the Sociology of Education*, pp. 241–268. New York: Greenwood.

Brettell, C. and Hollifield, J. eds (2008) *Migration Theory: Talking Across Disciplines*. New York: Routledge.

Brydon, D. (2013) Modes and models of postcolonial cross-disciplinarity. In Huggan, G. (ed.) *The Oxford Handbook of Postcolonial Studies*, pp. 427–448. Oxford: Oxford University Press.

Bryman, A. (2012) *Social Research Methods*. Oxford: Oxford University Press.

Byam, P. (1997) New Wine in a Very Old Bottle: Canadian Protestant Missionaries as Facilitators of Development in Central Angola 1886–1961. Ottawa: University of Ottawa, School of Graduate Studies, unpublished PhD thesis.

Cahen, M. (2012) 'Portugal is in the sky': Conceptual considerations on communities, Lusitanity and Lusophony. In Morier-Genoud and Cahen, M. (eds) *Imperial Migrations*, pp. 297–315. Basingstoke: Palgrave Macmillan.

Candeias, P., Malheiros, J., Marques, J.C. and Liberato, E. (2019) Portuguese emigration to Angola (2000–2015): strengthening a specific postcolonial relationship in a new global framework? In Pereira, C. and Azevedo, J. (eds) *New and Old Routes of Portuguese Emigration: Uncertain Futures at the Periphery of Europe*, pp. 209–238. Cham: Springer Open.

Castelo, C. (1998) *O Modo Português de Estar no Mundo: O Luso-Tropicalismo e a Ideologia Colonial Portuguesa (1933–1961)*. Porto: Edições Afrontamento.

Castles, S. and Delgado Wise, R. eds. (2008) *Migration and Development: Perspectives from the South*. Geneva: International Organization for Migration.

Castles, S. and Kosack, G. (1973) *Immigrant Workers and Class Structure in Western Europe*. London: Oxford University Press.

Castles, S. and Miller, M. (2009) *The Age of Migration*. New York: Palgrave Macmillan.

Chakrabarty, D. (2000) *Provincializing Europe*. Princeton and Oxford: Princeton University Press.

Chang, H. (2008) *Bad Samaritans*. New York: Bloomsbury Press.

Chavez, L. (2008) *The Latino Threat*. Stanford: Stanford University Press.

Cohen, R. ed. (1995) *The Cambridge Survey of World Migration*. Cambridge: Cambridge University Press.

Cohen, R. and Toninato, P. (2010) The creolization debate: analysing mixed identities and culture. In Cohen, R. and Toninato, P. (eds) *The Creolization Reader: Studies in Mixed Identities and Cultures*, pp. 1–22. London: Routledge.

Collier, P. (2013) *Exodus, Immigration and Multiculturalism in the 21st Century*. London: Allen Lane.

Comaroff, J. and Comaroff, J. (2001) Millennial capitalism: first thoughts on a second coming. In Comaroff, J. and Comaroff, J. (eds) *Millennial Capitalism and the Culture of Neoliberalism*, pp. 1–56. Durham NC and London: Duke University Press.

Comaroff, J. and Comaroff, J. (2012) *Theory from the South or How Euro-America is Evolving toward Africa*. London: Paradigm.

Connell, R. (2007) *Southern Theory: The Global Dynamics of Knowledge in Social Science*. Cambridge: Policy Press.

Corrado, J. (2008) *The Creole Elite and the Rise of Angolan Proto-Nationalism 1870–1920*. New York: Cambria Press.

Costa, J., Teixeira Lopes, J. and Louça, F. (2014) *Os Donos Angolanos de Portugal*. Lisbon: Bertrand Editora.

Crawley, H., Düvell, F.D., Jones, K., McMahon, S. and Sigona, N. (2018) *Unravelling Europe's 'Migration Crisis'*. Bristol: Policy Press.

Da Cruz, D. (2019) *Racismo o Machado Afiado em Angola*. Lisbon: Edições Rui Costa Pinto.

De Haas, H. (2008) *Migration and Development: A Theoretical Perspective*. Oxford: University of Oxford, International Migration Institute, Working Paper No. 9.

De Sousa Santos, B. (2002) Between Prospero and Caliban: colonialism, postcolonialism, and inter-identity. *Luso-Brazilian Review*, 39(2): 2–43.

Dølvik, J. (2013) European movement of labour: challenges for European social models. In Jurado, E. and Brochmann, G. (eds) *Europe's Immigration Challenge: Reconciling Work, Welfare and Mobility*, pp. 33–58. London: I.B. Tauris.

Duffy, J. (1962) *Portugal in Africa*. Baltimore: Penguin.

Emerson, M. Fretz, R. and Swaw, L. (1995) *Writing Ethnographic Fieldnotes*. Chicago: The University of Chicago Press.

Escobar, A. (1995) *Encountering Development: The Making and Unmaking of the Third World*. Princeton NJ: Princeton University Press.

Etounga-Manguelle, D. (2000) Does Africa need a cultural adjustment programme? In Harrison, L. and Huntington, S. (eds) *Culture Matters: How Values Shape Human Progress*, pp. 65–79. New York: Basic Books.

Fairclough, N. (1992) *Discourse and Social Change*. Cambridge: Polity Press.

Fanon, F. (1986) *Black Skin, White Masks*. London: Pluto Press.

Favell, A. (2008) Rebooting migration theory: interdisciplinarity, globality, and postdisciplinarity in migration studies. In Brettell, C. and Hollifield, J. (eds) *Migration Theory: Talking Across Disciplines*, pp. 259–278. New York: Routledge.

Favell, A. Feldblum, M. and Smith, P. (2009). The human face of global mobility: a research agenda. In Smith, M. and Favell, A. (eds) *The Human Face of Global Mobility: International Highly Skilled Migration in Europe, North America and the Asia-Pacific*, pp. 1–25. New Brunswick: Transaction Publishers.

Fechter, A. and Walsh, K. (2012) Examining 'expatriate' continuities: postcolonial approaches to mobile professionals. In Fechter, A. and Walsh, K. (eds) *The New Expatriates: Postcolonial Approaches to Mobile Professionals*, pp. 9–22. Abingdon: Routledge.

Ferguson, N. (2012) *Civilization: The West and the Rest*. London: Penguin.

Fikes, K. (2009) *Managing African Portugal*. Durham NC: Duke University Press.

Freyre, G. (1946) *The Masters and the Slaves. A Study in the Development of Brazilian Civilization*. New York: Alfred Knopf.

Freyre, G. (1961) *The Portuguese and the Tropics*. Lisbon: International Congress of the History of Discoveries.

Fukuyama, F. (1996) *Trust*. New York: Simon & Schuster.

Glick Schiller, N. and Faist, T. (2010) Migration, development and social transformation. In Glick Schiller, N. and Faist, T. (eds) *Migration, Development and Transnationalization*, pp. 1–21. New York: Berghahn.

Glorius, B. and Domínguez-Mujica, J. (2017) Introduction. In Glorius, B. and Domínguez-Mujica, J. (eds) *European Mobility in Times of Crisis: The New Context of European South-North Migration*. Bielefeld: transcript, 7–13.

Góis, P. and Marques, C. (2009) Portugal as a semi-peripheral country in the global migration system. *International Migration*, 47(3): 21–50.

Gopal, P. (2013) Renegade prophets and native acolytes: liberalism and imperialism today. In Huggan, G. (ed.) *The Oxford Handbook of Postcolonial Studies*, pp. 197–216. Oxford: Oxford University Press.

Grosfoguel, R. (2010) The epistemic decolonial turn: beyond political-economic paradigms. *Cultural Studies*, 21(2–3): 211–223.

Habti, D. and Elo, M. (2019) Rethinking self-initiated expatriates in international highly skilled migration. In Habti, D. and Elo, D. (eds) *Global Mobility of Highly Skilled People: Multidisciplinary Perspectives on Self-Initiated Expatriation*, pp. 1–40. Cham: Springer Open.

Hardwick, S. (2008) Space, place and pattern: geographical theories in international migration. In Brettell, C. and Hollifield, J. (eds) *Migration Theory: Talking Across Disciplines*, pp. 161–182. New York: Routledge.

Harrison, L. (2000) Introduction: why culture matters. In Harrison, L. and Huntington, S. (eds) *Culture Matters*, pp. xvii–xxxiii. New York: Basic Books.

Harvey, D. (2001) Cosmopolitanism and the banality of geographical evils. In Comaroff, J. and Comaroff, J. (eds) *Millennial Capitalism and the Culture of Neoliberalism*, pp. 271–310. Durham and London: Duke University Press.

Harvey, D. (2006) *Spaces of Global Capitalism: Towards a Theory of Uneven Geographical Development*. London: Verso.

Hatzky, C. (2012) *Cubans in Angola: South-South Cooperation and Transfer of Knowledge, 1976–1991*. Madison: The University of Wisconsin Press.

Hayes, M. (2014) 'We gained a lot over what we would have had': the geographical arbitrage of America's lifestyle migrants to Cuenca, Ecuador. *Journal of Ethnic and Migration Studies*, 40(12): 1953–1971.

Hayes, M. and Pérez-Gañán, R. (2017) North–South migrations and the asymmetric expulsions of late capitalism: global inequality, arbitrage, and new dynamics of North–South transnationalism. *Migration Studies*, 5(1): 116–135.

Henderson, L. (1979) *Angola: Five Centuries of Conflict*. Ithaca: Cornell University Press.

Henderson, L. (1990) *A Igrega em Angola: Um Rio com Várias Correntes*. Lisbon: Alem-Mar.

Herrnstein, R. and Murray, C. (1994) *The Bell Curve: Intelligence and Class Structure in American Life*. New York: Simon & Schuster.

Heywood, L. (1989) *Unita* and ethnic nationalism in Angola. *The Journal of Modern African Studies*, 27(1): 47–66.

Hodges, T. (2004) *Angola: Anatomy of an Oil State*. Bloomington: Indiana University Press.

Holland, S. (1979) Dependent development: Portugal as periphery. In Seers, D., Schaffer, B. and Kiljunen, L. (eds) *Underdeveloped Europe: Studies in Core–Periphery Relations*, pp. 139–160. Hassocks: Harvester Press.

Huntington, S. (1996) *The Clash of Civilizations*. New York: Simon and Schuster.

Huntington, S. (2004) *Who Are We?* New York: Simon and Schuster.

IOM (2013) *World Migration Report 2013: Migrant Well-Being and Development*. Geneva: International Organization for Migration.

IOM (2020) *World Migration Report 2020*. Geneva: International Organization for Migration.

Jerónimo, M. (2015) *The 'Civilizing Mission' of Portuguese Colonialism, 1870–1930*. Basingstoke: Palgrave Macmillan.

Jørgensen, M. and Phillips, L. (2002) *Discourse Analysis as Theory and Method*. London: Sage.

Kaplan, R. (2000) *The Coming Anarchy*. New York: Random House.

King, R. (2012) Geography and migration studies: retrospect and prospect. *Population, Space and Place*, 18(2): 134–153.

King, R. (2015) Migration and Southern Europe – a center-periphery dynamic? In Baumeister, M. and Sala, R. (eds) *Southern Europe? Italy, Spain, Portugal and Greece from the 1950s to the Present Day*, pp. 139–169. Frankfurt: Campus Verlag.

King, R. (2019) New migration dynamics on the south-western periphery of Europe: theoretical reflections on the Portuguese case. In Azevedo, J. and Pereira, C. (eds) *New and Old Routes of Portuguese Migration: Uncertain Futures at the Periphery of Europe*, pp. 267–281. Cham: Springer.

Klekowski Von Koppenfels, A. (2014) *Migrants or Expatriates? Americans in Europe*. London: Palgrave Macmillan.

Kritz, M., Zlotnik, H. and Lim, L. (1992) *International Migration Systems: A Global Approach*. Oxford: Clarendon Press.

Krug, J. (2011) The strange life of lusotropicalism in Luanda: on race, nationality, gender, and sexuality in Angola. In Talton, B. and Mills, T. (eds) *Black Subjects in Africa and its Diasporas*, pp. 109–127. New York: Palgrave Macmillan.

Lafleur, J.M. and Stanek, M. (2017a) *South-North Migration of EU Citizens at Times of Crisis*. Cham: Springer Open.

Lafleur, J.M. and Stanek, M. (2017b) EU migration and economic crisis: concepts and issues. In Lafleur, J. and Stanek, M. (eds) *South-North Migration of EU Citizens in Times of Crisis*, pp. 1–14 . Cham: Springer Open.

Latouche, S. (1996) *Westernization of the World: The Significance, Scope and Limits of the Drive towards Global Uniformity*. Cambridge: Polity Press.

Lentz, C. (2013) *Land, Mobility, and Belonging in West Africa*. Bloomington: Indiana University Press.

Loomba, A. (2005) *Colonialism/Postcolonialism*. Abingdon: Routledge.

Luce, F. (1990) A History of Labour in Angola. Toronto: University of Toronto, unpublished LLM thesis.

Lundström, C. (2014) *White Migrations: Gender, Whiteness and Privilege in Transnational Migration*. New York: Palgrave Macmillan.

Mabeko-Tali, J. (2018) *Guerrilhas e Lutas Socias o MPLA Perante Si Proprio 1960–1977*. Lisbon: Mercado de Letras Editores.

Macamo, E. (2005) Denying modernity: the regulation of native labour in colonial Mozambique and its postcolonial aftermath. In Macamo, E. (ed.) *Negotiating Modernity: Africa's Ambivalent Experience*, pp. 67–97. Dakar: Codesria.

Malaquias, A. (2000) Ethnicity and conflict in Angola: prospects for reconciliation. In Cilliers, J. and Dietrich, C. (eds) *Angola's War Economy: The Role of Oil and Diamonds*, 95–113. Pretoria: Institute for Security Studies.

Malaquias, A. (2007) *Rebels and Robbers: Violence in Postcolonial Angola*. Uppsala: Nordiska Afrikainstitute.

Maldonado-Torres, N. (2010) On the coloniality of being: contributions to the development of a concept. In Mignolo, W.D. and Escobar, A. (eds) *Globalization and the Decolonial Option*, pp. 94–123. New York: Routledge.

Malheiros, J. (2005) Jogos de relações internacionais: repensar a posição de Portugal no arquipélago migratório global. In Barreto, A. (ed.) *Globalização e Migrações*, pp. 251–272. Lisbon: Imprensa de Ciências Sociais.

Mamdani, M. (1996) *Citizen and Subject: Contemporary Africa and the Legacy of Late Colonialism*. Princeton: Princeton University Press.

Marques, J. and Góis, P. (2017) Structural emigration: the revival of Portuguese outflows. In Lafleur, J. and Stanek, M. (eds) *South-North Migration of EU Citizens at Times of Crisis*, pp. 65–82. Cham: Springer Open.

Massey, D. (1993) Power geometry and a progressive sense of place. In Bird, J., Curtis, B., Putnam, T., Robertson, G. and Tickner, L. (eds) *Mapping the Futures: Local Cultures, Global Change*, pp. 59–69. London: Routledge.

Massey, D. (2005) *For Space*. London: Sage.

Massey, D., Arango, J., Hugo, G., Kouaouci, A., Pellegrino, A. and Taylor, J.E. (2006) Theories of international migration: a review and appraisal. In Massina, A. and Lehav, G. (eds) *The Migration Reader: Exploring Politics and Policies*, pp. 34–62. London: Lynne Rienner.

Mbembe, A. (2001) *On the Postcolony*. Berkeley: University of California Press.

McEwan, C. (2009) *Postcolonialism and Development*. London: Routledge.

McIntosh, P. (1989) White privilege: unpacking the invisible knapsack. *Peace and Freedom Magazine*, pp. 10–12.

McLeod, J. (2000) *Beginning Postcolonialism*. Manchester: Manchester University Press.

Mignolo, W. (2000) *Local Histories/Global Designs. Coloniality, Subaltern Knowledges and Border Thinking*. Princeton: Princeton University Press.

Mignolo, W. (2011) *The Dark Side of Western Modernity*. Durham NC: Duke University Press.

Moco, M. (2015) *Angola Estado da Nação ou Etnia Politica*. Lisbon: Marmoco Criações.

Morier-Genoud, E. and Cahen, M. (2013) Introduction: Portugal, empire and migrations – was there ever an autonomous social imperial space? In Morier-Genoud, E. and Cahen, M. (eds) *Imperial Migrations: Colonial Communities and Diaspora in the Portuguese World*, pp. 1–30. Basingstoke: Palgrave Macmillan.

Moss, P. (2002) *Feminist Geography in Practice: Research and Methods*. Oxford: Blackwell.

Mudimbe, V. (1988) *The Invention of Africa: Gnosis, Philosophy and the Order of Knowledge*. Bloomington. Indiana University Press.

Nascimento, W. (2016) Entre assimilados, mulheres e homens do mato: a busca pelo sujeito nacional em luadino vieira. *História Questões e Debates Curitiba*, 64(1): 227–298.

Observatório de Emigração (2019) http://observatorioemigracao.pt/np4EN/paises.html?id=9.

O'Reilly, K. (2005) *Ethnographic Methods*. Abingdon: Routledge.

Pawson, L. (2014) *In the Name of the People*. London: I.B. Tauris.

Pereira, S. (2010) *Trabalhadores de Origem Africana em Portugal. Impacto das Novas Vagas de Imigração*. Lisbon: Edições Colibri.

Pereira, C. and Azevedo, J. (2019) The fourth wave of Portuguese emigration: austerity policies, European peripheries and postcolonial continuities. In Pereira, C. and Azevedo, J. (eds) *New and Old Routes of Portuguese Emigration: Uncertain Futures at the Periphery of Europe*, pp. 1–26. Cham: Springer Open.

Piore, M. (1979) *Birds of Passage: Migrant Labor and Industrial Societies*. Cambridge: Cambridge University Press.

Portes, A. (1998) Social capital: its origins and applications in modern sociology. *Annual Review of Sociology, 24*: 1–24.

Power, M. (2003) *Rethinking Development Geographies*. London: Routledge.

Power, M. (2006) Anti-racism, deconstruction and 'overdevelopment'. *Progress in Development Studies*, 6(1): 24–39.

Quijano, A. (2010) Coloniality and modernity/rationality. In Mignolo, W. and Escobar, A. (eds) *Globalization and the Decolonial Option*, pp. 22–32. New York: Routledge.

Saïd, E. (1978) *Orientalism*. London: Routledge and Kegan Paul.

Samers, M. (1997) The production of diaspora: Algerian emigrants from colonialism to neo-colonialism (1840–1940). *Antipode*, 29(1): 32–64.

Sawyer, M. (2006) *Racial Politics in Post-Revolutionary Cuba*. Cambridge: Cambridge University Press.

Sayyid, S. (2013) Empire, Islam and the postcolonial. In Huggan, G. (ed.) *The Oxford Handbook of Postcolonial Studies*, pp. 127–142. Oxford: Oxford University Press.

Schmitz, C.M. (2018) Performing 'China in Africa' for the West: Chinese migrant discourses in Angola. *Asian and Pacific Migration Journal*, 27(1): 9–27.

Schubert, J. (2017) *Working the System. A Political Ethnography of the New Angola*. Ithaca and London: Cornell University Press.

Seers, D. (1979) The periphery of Europe. In Seers, D., Schaffer, B. and Kiljunen, L. (eds) *Underdeveloped Europe: Studies in Core–Periphery Relations*, pp. 3–34. Hassocks: Harvester Press.

Sen, A. (1999) *Development as Freedom*. Oxford: Oxford University Press.

Sen, A. (2006) *Identity and Violence: The Illusion of Destiny*. London: Penguin.

Serrado, R. (2012) *O Estado Novo e o Futebol*. Northbrook: Prime Publishing.

Shohat, L. and Stam, S. (1994) *Unthinking Eurocentrism*. London: Routledge.

Slater, D. (2004) *Geopolitics and the Postcolonial*. Oxford: Blackwell.

Smith, R. (2006) *Mexican New York: Transnational Lives of New Immigrants*. Berkeley: University of California Press.

Smith, S. (2019) *The Scramble for Europe: Young Africa on its Way to the Old Continent*. Cambridge: Polity Press.

Soares de Oliveira, R. (2015) *Magnificent and Beggar Land: Angola since the Civil War*. London: Hurst.

Soremekun, F. (1965) A History of the American Board of Missions in Angola 1880–1940. Evanston: Northwestern University, unpublished PhD thesis.

Sultana, F. (2007) Reflexivity, positionality and participatory ethics: negotiating fieldwork dilemmas in international research. ACME*: An International Journal for Critical Geographies*, 6(3): 374–385.

Suri, H. (2011) Purposeful sampling in qualitative research synthesis. *Qualitative Research Journal*, 11(2): 63–75.

Torfing, J. (1999) *New Theories of Discourse*. Oxford: Blackwell.

Twine, F. (2000) *Racism in a Racial Democracy*. New Jersey: Rutgers University Press.

Vala, J., Lopes, D. and Lima, M. (2008) Black immigrants in Portugal: Luso-tropicalism and prejudices. *Journal of Social Issues*, 64(2): 287–302.

Van der Waals, W. (2011) *Portugal's War in Angola 1961–1974*. Pretoria: Protea Book House.

Vaughan-Williams, N. (2015) *Europe's Border Crisis: Biopolitical Security and Beyond*. Oxford: Oxford University Press.

Vertovec, S. and Wessendorf, S. (2010) Introduction: assessing the backlash against multiculturalism in Europe. In Vertovec, S. and Wessendorf, S. (eds) *The Multiculturalism Backlash: European Discourses, Policies and Practices*, pp. 1–31. Abingdon: Routledge.

Vradis, A., Papada, E., Painter, J. and Papoutsi, A. (2019) *New Borders: Hotspots and the European Migration Regime*. London: Pluto Press.

Waldorff, P. (2017) Renegotiated (post-)colonial relations within the new Portuguese migration to Angola. *Africa Spectrum* 52(3): 55–80.

Wallerstein, I. (1976) *The Modern World System*. New York: Academic Press.

Wallerstein, I. (1995) *After Liberalism*. New York: The New Press.

Walsh, K. (2018) *Transnational Geographies of the Heart*. Chichester: Wiley.

Warwick, A. (2003) *The Cultivation of Whiteness: Science, Health and Racial Destiny in Australia*. New York: Basic Books.

White, S. (2002) Thinking race, thinking development. *Third World Quarterly*, 23(3): 407–417.

Williams, G., Meth, P. and Willis, K. (2014) *Geographies of Developing Areas: The Global South in a Changing World*. Abingdon: Routledge.

Appendix

	Name/ Gender	Profession/ Qualification	Nationality/ Race	Place/Month/ Year of Interview
1	Abel (M)	Consultant, lecturer/ PhD	Angolan/Black	Lubango, October 2015
2	Ana-Maria (F)	University lecturer/ Bachelor	Portuguese/White	Lubango, September 2015
3	Alfredo (M)	Politician/Bachelor	Angolan/Black	Lubango, September 2015
4	Antonio (M)	Immigration official/ Bachelor	Angolan/Black	Lubango, October 2015
5	Bety (F)	Economist/Bachelor	Angolan/Black	Lubango, September 2015
6	Borges (M)	Lecturer/MA	Portuguese retornado/White	Lubango, October 2015
7	Brito (M)	Medical Doctor	Portuguese/White	Lisbon, July 2016
8	Carlos (M)	Professor/PhD	Portuguese/White	Lisbon, July 2016
9	Carlita (F)	Civil engineer/ Bachelor	Portuguese/White	Lisbon, August 2016
10	Catarina (F)	Secretary/technical training	Portuguese-Angolan/White	Lubango, October 2015
11	Cecilia (F)	Teacher/Bachelor	Portuguese/White	Lubango, October 2015
12	Daniel (M)	Business/technical training	Angolan/Black	Lubango, October 2015
13	David (M)	Professor/PhD	Portuguese/White	Lisbon, July 2016
14	Deolinda (F)	Horse-riding instructor/technical training	Portuguese/White	Lubango, September 2015
15	Ernesto (M)	Business/technical training	Portuguese/White	Lubango, August 2015
16	Fernando (M)	Mechanic/technical training	Portuguese/White	Lubango, October 2015

	Name/ Gender	Profession/ Qualification	Nationality/ Race	Place/Month/ Year of Interview
17	Filipe (M)	Builder/technical training	Portuguese/White	Lubango, August 2015
18	Joao (M)	Builder/technical training	Portuguese/White	Lubango, August 2015
19	Jose (M)	Civil Engineer/ Bachelor	Portuguese retornado/White	Lisbon, July 2016
20	Jorge (M)	Manager/Bachelor	Angolan/Black	Lubango, October 2015
21	Justino (M)	Manager/MBA	Portuguese/White	Lubango, October 2015
22	Laurinda (F)	Lecture/Bachelor	Portuguese/White	Lubango, October 2015
23	Lopes (M)	Lecturer/MA	Portuguese/White	Lubango, September 2015
24	Luis (M)	Builder/technical training	Portuguese/White	Lubango, September 2015
25	Maria (F)	Manager/Economist	Angolan/White	Lubango, August 2015
26	Mario (M)	Lecturer/PhD	Portuguese/White	Lisbon, July 2016
27	Martinho (M)	Professor/PhD	Portuguese/White	Lisbon, July 2016
28	Miguel (M)	Builder/technical training	Portuguese/White	Lubango, August 2015
29	Nadia (F)	Teacher/Bachelor	Portuguese/White	Lubango, September 2015
30	Paula (F)	Cashier/technical training	Portuguese/White	Lubango, October 2015
31	Pedro (M)	Administrator	Angolan/Black	Lubango, August 2015
32	Pedroto (M)	Lecturer/MA	Angolan/Black	Lubango, September 2015
33	Rafaela (F)	Nurse/Bachelor	Portuguese/White	Lisbon, August 2016
34	Raul (M)	Civil Engineer/ Bachelor	Portuguese/White	Lisbon, August 2016
35	Romana (F)	Lecturer/PhD	Portuguese-Angola/White	Lubango, August 2015

	Name/ Gender	Profession/ Qualification	Nationality/ Race	Place/Month/ Year of Interview
36	Rosalia (F)	Manager/Bachelor	Angola/White	Lubango, October 2016
37	Sabina (F)	Beauty Salon/technical training	Portuguese/White	Lubango, September 2015
38	Sofia (F)	Manager/technical training	Portuguese/White	Lubango, September 2015
39	Solange (F)	Lecturer/MA	Angolan/Black	Lubango, October 2015
40	Tamara (F)	Teacher/Bachelor	Portuguese/White	Lubango, August 2015
41	Teresa (F)	Manager/technical training	Portuguese/White	Lubango, October 2015
42	Tomas (M)	Business/Bachelor	Angola/Black	Lubango, September 2015
43	Valter (M)	Manager/technical training	Portuguese/White	Lubango, August 2015
44	Vera (M)	Lecturer/Bachelor	Portuguese/White	Lubango, September 2015
45	Zarito (M)	Builder/technical training	Portuguese/White	Lisbon, August 2016

Note: Some of the participants with technical training have not completed tertiary education. Some have also learned their trade on the job without ever attending any training. Second, some of the participants were born in Angola but left at an early age and identify themselves as Portuguese. For those participants, I included the word '*retornado*'.

Bereits erschienen in der Reihe „Bayreuther Studien zu Politik und Gesellschaft in Afrika"
Already published in the series "Bayreuth Studies in African Politics and Societies"

North to South Migration
Portuguese Labour Migration to Angola
by Asaf Augusto,
2021, Volume 10

The Making of a Petro-State
Governmentality and Development Practice in Uganda's Albertine Graben
by Paddy Kinyera,
2020, Volume 7

Diversity Gains
Stepping Stones and Pitfalls
edited by Sarah Böllinger, Carsten Mildner, Ulf Vierke,
2020, Volume 6

Die Welt aus der Perspektive der Entwicklungssoziologie
Festschrift für Dieter Neubert
edited by Artur Bogner, Reinhart Kößler, Rüdiger Korff, Henning Melber,
2020, Band 5

Medialisierungen Afrikas
edited by Valerie Hänsch, Johanna Rieß, Ivo Ritzer, Heike Wagner,
2018, Volume 4

Local State Institutional Reforms in Ghana
Actors, Legitimacy and the Unfulfilled Promise of Participatory Development
by Matthew Sabbi,
2017, Volume 3

Mittelklassen, Mittelschichten oder Milieus in Afrika?
Gesellschaften im Wandel
edited by Antje Daniel, Sebastian Müller, Florian Stoll, Rainer Öhlschläger,
2016, Volume 2

Globale Krisen – Lokale Konflikte?
Soziale Bewegungen in Afrika
edited by Bettina Engels, Melanie Müller, Rainer Öhlschläger,
2015, Volume 1